THE
BARE
NAKED
TRUTH

Bekah Hamrick Martin

THE BARE NAKED TRUTH

Dating, Waiting, and God's Purity Plan

ZONDERVAN®

ZONDERVAN.com/
AUTHORTRACKER
follow your favorite authors

To Ethan,
Because you know my bare naked
thoughts, feelings, fears —
and love me
in spite of them.
Thanks for waiting for me.

Contents

Acknowledgments

THE GIRLS AND GUYS who share their stories in this book: you have been brave — and probably a little foolish. Thank you for your candor.

The Tiny Human, for not reporting me for child neglect. You can have your mom back now (at least until the next book).

Rachel Kent, Wendy Lawton, and of course, Janet Grant, for seeing past the booger in my nose at our first meeting. Also for years of standing by me and my ideas ("What about a book where I say *naked* as many times as possible?").

Jacque Alberta, for believing I could write on 1.5 hours of sleep. For blessing me with the craziest, most dream-fulfilling year of my life. And for making writing the most ridiculously fun it could be.

My parents, Randy and Merry Hamrick, for forgiving me for writing a book with the word *naked* in the title.

Ethan's parents, Bill and Sue Martin, for giving me your son — against your better judgment. And for helping the Tiny Human through the emotional aspects of having two artistic parents.

My sibs, Molly and Philip, for signing releases that promised you wouldn't sue me for these stories. Remember the releases? Remember?

Cecil Murphey, for investing in the dreams of so many writers — more specifically, mine.

Suzie Eller, for threatening me until I talked to an agent. Also for mentoring me through countless book proposals (which were more intense than marriage proposals).

Steve Parolini, for months of panicked email messages, phone calls, and general neediness. From me to you, I mean.

Halee Matthews, for keeping me organized on the fly. And not on the fly. And pretty much all the time. Also for your editing expertise, which has left me a much stronger and generally more hospitalized writer.

Abbie Miller, for having more talent in your little eyelash than I have in my whole body — and using it to manage realteenfaith.com in my absence. (Your talent, not your eyelash.)

Annette Dammer, for telling me a book is written one email at a time. I promise to stop filling your inbox — for a few days anyway.

Lisa, Nancy, and Christina Hale, for keeping my child from feeling like an orphan while I worked with the "other baby." Because of you, I will save on Zoey's therapy in her later years.

My extended family, for never getting tired of hearing me talk about "the book." Or at least for not chucking the free copy you'll get at the end of this.

I love you all. And that's the bare naked truth.

Introduction

THE WORDS *BARE NAKED* still send chills down my spine — but not in the way you might expect. Yes, I am married to a hot boy.[1] For some reason, though, when I hear the words *bare naked*, I don't always think about my hot boy.

Sometimes I think about that terrible day last fall. I think about the moment before I got naked. I think about the moment before I, the ever-mature camp counselor, walked through the minefield of sleeping girls and hoped … prayed … and plotted.

This was it. No more Mrs. Nice Guy. No more standing by while the other girls stole the hot water for their early-morning showers. It was time for *me* to be the water-hog. I was going to help these campers fulfill their dreams of world travel (to Iceland).

My heart pounded as I slipped past the girls and pushed open the bathroom door. The clock on the counter blinked seven a.m. I listened closely: no water running. Was this revenge story too good to be true?

Pretty much.

What I tell you next is not something I usually talk about in mixed company, because my mama raised me in the South, where you don't use words like I'm about to use. But because we're all girls here, I'm just gonna put it bluntly: I stripped.

And then I realized there was no place to put my pjs. The floor was still soaked from the previous night's showers. Going back for another towel to mop it up meant letting those water stealers beat me to the shower. Again.

I knew what I had to do: protect my pjs by hanging them on

---

1. See www.bekahhamrickmartin.com for evidence. But remember—he's mine.

the shower curtain. Only one problem: turns out shower rods aren't designed to support the weight of clothing.[2]

So when gravity began to take its course, we were all surprised — myself and the three blonde cheerleaders lined up to be next in the shower, who were squealing in a way I'd never heard them squeal before, and in a way that had nothing to do with cold water.

Friends, I'm just gonna be honest here: there is no pretty way to put up a shower curtain when you're naked. You find yourself asking life-altering questions like *Do I like my butt best, or my boobs? Which side is less likely to make these cheerleaders cringe?*

I'm not gonna lie. People saw things they didn't want to see. But let me tell ya, we had it all out in the open.

It may not always be pretty, but sometimes (when it doesn't involve a camp bathroom and perfect-bodied cheerleaders) out in the open is the best way to go. And because of that, I've decided to take that approach with this book — the bare naked one.

This book is just the truth. Okay — with a little craziness mixed in. I'm not afraid to talk about the tough questions — the ones teens ask me every day. Questions like:

- How far is too far?
- Is there anything wrong with masturbation?
- What do guys really want in a girl?
- What are the advantages to waiting for sex?
- What are the disadvantages to waiting?

When it comes to bare naked truth, I won't be hiding behind polite words or Sunday school stories in this book. The question is, can you handle it, or are you gonna run screaming like a girl?

I'll see you on the bare side.

Bekah

---

2. The rod tumbled faster than a two-ton rock avalanche.

LIE #1

I Have All the Sex Facts

I'M NOT SURE IF it was the crash or the blood-curdling scream that brought me to my knees. Two months after 9/11, I was sure I was on a plane with a group of terrorists. I sat there staring, shaking, wondering.

So this was it: my final moment. I'd always wondered if I would be heroic and strong. But the only strong thing was the sound of my heartbeat in my ears. And my breath. Maybe I could take these guys down with that.

It was all happening so fast I could barely respond. One moment the "terrorists" sat in their seats, quiet and subdued. The next moment they hit the floor, shouting and crowding around some unknown device.

Which turned out to be a digital camera — apparently a very expensive item — that they had dropped.[1] And we all know that screaming in a foreign language on an airplane after 9/11 about a dropped digital camera is a perfectly sensible thing to do.

BaRe NaKeD tip

Get all the information. (Duh.)

After a few hours, when I crawled out from under my seat,[2] I realized … things aren't always as they seem.

I thought I knew all the details of the situation. But if I'd known it was a digital camera hitting the floor, I could have avoided the whole being-bribed-by-an-airline-attendant-with-a-cookie-to-get-out-from-under-my-seat thing.

But no. I was operating only on the information I'd been given.

I can't believe I'm admitting this, but I did it again yesterday. Not the whole terrorists-on-an-airplane thing — just the failure to get all the details.

It all started because I'd always wanted cute eyebrows like other girls. You know — the kind that curve and then come down perfectly in just the right spot. My eyebrows wander haphazardly across my forehead like a village of lost caterpillars.

"Don't do it," my friend Katie[3] warned when I told her I wanted to fix my brows. "Don't touch them." Katie and I have been friends since we were three years old. She has seen the effects of my impulsive self-makeovers.

"Do you not remember the perm that made you look like Willy Wonka?" she asked. "Or the spray-on tan that turned you into a crunchy carrot stick?"

---

1. Hence the screaming.
2. Where *do* you go when there's a bomb in an airplane?
3. Here's the part where I should tell you some names in this book have been changed. Katie's is not one of them. (She didn't pay me enough.)

"But …"

"I'm telling you," she said, "leave this to the professionals."

"Leave this to the professionals," I repeated to myself as I walked into the salon. "Leave this to the professionals." Somehow those words brought comfort to my heart. *Professionals know what they're doing, right?*

"Waxing?" the man behind the counter asked when he took one look at my caterpillars.

"Yes. How'd you …?"

"Right this way."

The room he led me to was scarier than anything I'd ever seen in a spy-interrogation movie.[4]

"Lie down," the woman with the hot wax said. You read that correctly. She told me to lie down.

"Excuse me?" I said. "What is this? Surgery?"

"No speak English," she said. "Lie down."

I made her job easy, because with the words "No speak English," every hair on my entire body stood on end. *Rip!* Within sixty seconds, my face stung like I'd spent two days on the beach without sunscreen.

"Did you leave my eyelashes?" I asked.

Hot Wax Lady eyed me suspiciously as she plopped the mirror into my lap. Shakily, I picked it up and stared.

"You like?" she asked, smiling.

"I … I … I …" I tried to breathe.

It's a good thing I was lying down.

I'd never seen anything like it. Tiny strands of hair wandered aimlessly above my eyelids. Everything else was gone. Gone. I didn't like the caterpillars, but they were better than the little line of picnic ants now wandering across my skull.

---

4. There was a table. With straps.

My puffy eyes welled with tears. How could I ever show my face in public again?

"Looks nice," Hot Wax Lady proclaimed. "Seven dollars."

It's been an entire day since I almost slugged Hot Wax Lady. But even though I had a right to be mad at her, I also had a right to be mad at myself. I'd failed to ask the woman some very important questions. Questions like "Are you insured? Have you ever done this before? And you do realize I want some hair left over, right?"

It may sound crazy that I would let anyone touch my eyebrows when we couldn't even communicate, or that I'd crawl under my seat just because a camera hit the floor on an airplane. But we all make gut-impulse decisions every day. We decide who to hang out with, where to go, and what to do based on a few facts. We might even decide which bubbles to fill in on a test based on just a few minutes of studying.[5]

But what we're talking about in this book — the issue of keeping our legs crossed (or not) — is a bigger issue than our usual everyday decisions. As you know, sex isn't something to do or not to do just based on a few sources. Eyebrows grow back, but this whole sex thing — it has the potential to affect the rest of our lives.[6]

I don't know why you've decided what you've decided about sex up to this point. I do know that in high school I didn't set out to decide the sex issue for myself. For the first few years of high school, the topic kind of decided itself for me.[7]

But one day I was faced with the decision. And I knew I didn't want to make a half-informed one. Don't get me wrong — I knew what sex meant physically. I knew the risks, and I knew the benefits. I knew about STDs and pregnancies and — *ahhhh!* — orgasms. But what I was worried about was how I would feel emotionally after sex.

---

5. And if one of my English teachers is reading this, please don't take that as a confession.
6. Thankfully, it's not exactly boring test material.
7. Let's just say I wasn't on the top of the "hottest girls" list.

Was it just me, or did the high not seem to last very long for my friends? Was it just me, or was that heartbreak in their eyes? Was it just me, or did the majority of my friends struggle with feelings of emptiness and depression, even when they'd agreed with their partners beforehand that they would just be "friends with benefits"?

Think first. Act second.

I had to know.

It turned out it wasn't just me. I'll keep this short, but study after study shows the emotional effects of multiple sexual relationships for teen girls:

- Due to the bonding properties of dopamine and oxytocin released during sex, you can actually lose your ability to bond to your future spouse if you bond with multiple sexual partners beforehand (McIlhaney and Bush 2008).[a]
- Sexual baggage can cause distrust and fear in future relationships (Maher 2008).[b]
- Having multiple sexual partners actually increases your future risk of divorce (Maher 2008).[c]
- Seeking love through sex leaves many teens, especially girls, in emotional turmoil afterward (Meeker 2002).[d]
- Premarital sex increases a teen girl's risk of suicide by three times (U.S. Department of Health and Human Services 1994).[e]
- Early sexual activity could prevent girls from developing academically (Rector and Johnson 2005).[f]

My friend Camy, who is now a successful writer and biologist — a brilliant person — somehow overlooked studies like this when she was in high school. But don't let me spoil it for you — she wants to tell you in her own words.

SPOTLIGHT
Camy Tang

I'd always been top of my class in school. So I knew all about sex. What I didn't know about was love and relationships.

I knew the *major* stuff like:

A. Avoid getting pregnant like *those* girls in my class.
B. Avoid the violent guys who'd give you a black eye and broken arm.
C. Make sure the guy has a car.

And then there were the other things to keep in mind:

D. Make sure he respects you and doesn't talk down to you.
E. Make sure he understands up front what you are and are not willing to do.
F. Make sure he's always honest and transparent with you.
G. Make sure he's not too freaky-close to his mother.

That's all I really needed to know, right?

The problem was that the Christians in my life didn't like talking about sex. So I never understood the true spiritual nature of sex between a married couple. I didn't know sex *had* a spiritual component.

The truth is, God is spirit and God created sex, so of course sex has a spiritual component.

Sex is still a mystery to people, because while we can understand all the chemical, hormonal, and physical things about sex, there's a part of our souls involved, and that can't be measured. It's a part of us that only God knows and understands. And when I gave a piece of my soul away to a boy I wasn't married to, it caused damage that I can never undo.

So while I knew all about sex and all about consequences, there were still some things that took me by surprise.

And knowing about sex didn't prevent me from making bad

choices. *Knowledge doesn't necessarily keep you on the right path.* Only God can do that.

So while you might know a lot more about sex than you want to admit to your parents or your youth leader, it doesn't matter what you know or don't know. What matters is if you've completely surrendered your will to God so that he can give you the strength to make the right choices, to withstand temptation, and to walk away from a potentially bad situation, relationship, or conversation.

There are always things you don't yet know.

* * *

Like Camy, I noticed a lot of my friends struggling emotionally after sex. Some of you "experienced" girls are saying, "Whoa, back up. When I decided to have sex, I just did it because it felt good, or because my boyfriend pressured me, or because _____ (you fill in the blank)."

Let me just say I understand. I've made a lot of decisions before I had all the facts,[8] and we're not just talking about stuff like waxing eyebrows or hiding under airplane seats. We're talking about decisions that rocked my world, decisions that shattered my security, decisions I felt I could never recover from.

So if you look at this list of potential problems and you feel overwhelmed, can I tell you it's gonna be okay? I know a God who believes in second, third, fourth — infinite — chances. I know a God who overflows with grace and mercy. I know a God who wants to heal and restore every area of your life, just like he's healed and restored my life. (To learn more about that, keep reading.)

But in order to be restored, we need to recognize that *knowing all the facts* is a lie. We need to realize that maybe, just maybe, our friends' perceptions of these facts could be a little skewed. We need

---

8. I'll be sharing more of those later in the book.

to throw away every preconceived notion that sex is no big deal and realize that this decision — to cross or uncross our legs — is not as casual as we might feel. And we need to realize our fears play a big role in whether we decide to wait. Just like my fears affected my Big Decision.[9]

Be Afraid — Very Afraid. Or Not.

Last weekend my man and I made the Big Decision. It was somewhere up there with the *Should we have kids?* decision.

You guessed it. It was huge.

We made the *Should we go camping?* decision.

We've talked about the *Should we go camping?* decision for the past two years. Usually these talks resemble Middle East peace talks — not because we're hostile (we're not), but because both parties realize we're discussing something that only one of the parties wants to do.

Until now.

Aliens must have invaded my brain. There is no other explanation for why an always pedicured, manicured, and perfumicured girl would suggest, "Honey, you wanna spend a night alone in the woods?"

Of course — what was he going to say? The bags were in the car within three point five seconds. One hour later we were at the campsite. Well, at least part of me was at the campsite. The other half of me had to psychologically detach from the horrible scene.

There it was — right before my very eyes — a patch of dirt.

"This … this … this … is it?" I asked.

"This is it!" he said excitedly. "Let's get some firewood."

This is where this story becomes useful to you, my dear reader.

---

9. Note the sarcasm.

I would now like to explain how to collect firewood the next time you're in the woods:

1. Pick up stick.
2. Pick up another stick.
3. Repeat for thirty minutes until you have a fire that will burn for approximately fifteen and a half seconds.
4. Salvage all the wood from the fort in the forest and silently apologize to whatever kid built it, all the while hoping that the builder wasn't actually an ax murderer who uses it as shelter while preying on his camping victims.

Speaking of ax murderers, I have to admit the thought crossed my mind as the sun went down. Not the thought to ax murder my husband (after all, I was the one who finally surrendered to this camping idea). Rather, the thought that maybe — just maybe — the fort was built by someone who was up to no good. Just as I had that thought … it happened.

A twig snapped. A shadow moved between the trees. My heart quivered. The shadow moved closer and closer … until finally the figure stepped into the moonlight.

"Well, folks," said the park ranger, "it looks like you're all alone tonight. No one else in the park. I'll lock the gate behind me."

No! I wanted to shout. *Don't leave us here!* Suddenly, I felt like a caged animal. What were we thinking? What were we doing? We were all alone on a patch of dirt in the middle of a bathroom-for-saken state park.

It was a long night. Every twig that snapped, every owl that hooted, every breeze that blew made my heart pound faster. It was not romantic; it was the most terrifying night of my life. I decided, at exactly 2:42 a.m., that this was the one — and only — time I would ever go camping.

I may be a risk taker when it comes to eyebrow waxing, but when we're talking about camping, I am clearly a complete, total, and utter wuss. I have to admit that I made my decision never to camp again based on that fear — which is why I told you this story.

Because fear is no way to make the *actual* big decisions in life.

A lot of books are going to try to scare you into their point of view. That's not my plan here. I want you to make decisions about sex based on the fact that you are intelligent, not scared. I want you to make decisions about sex based on facts. The real ones. Ones like my friend Annie used to make smart decisions for herself.

SPOTLIGHT
Annie Downs

"I may not be right, but I'm always sure." My friend Dave says something like that, but I think I'm butchering the quote. The idea is the same, and I totally do it too: whether I know the right answer, I speak confidently in the direction I think is right, and people believe me.

Scary, I know.

I mean, I don't do it on important things. I just do it on random information, like facts about child actors from the '90s — "I'm sure Mary-Kate is the older one" — or recipe measurements — "Yeah, if you add three tablespoons of sugar, that is *just* like a cup."

I lead a small group of college girls for my church, and last night as we sat around my living room eating Mexican seven-layer dip, we talked about boys. They asked questions, and I answered. Then one girl asked, "What if you're wrong, Annie?" Her eyes said a million things. She needed pure truth. And full truth. She needed all the facts.

In those moments, saying anything but the full truth would be detrimental. When the chips are down, I know I'd better have the facts. Like, really really.

Sometimes we think we know it all. I do, at least. But whether the subject is God or relationships or life in general, it doesn't do us any good to act like we know everything when we haven't checked out the facts.

Because unfortunately, we don't know everything there is to know about everything.

When you hear that in your head — *that you know everything there is to know* — it's a lie.

(Just for the record, Ashley is older, and it takes sixteen tablespoons to equal a cup. And that's the truth.)

* * *

Like Annie, I will do my best to share those facts bare naked — for good or for bad. Because, really, there's a big difference between an ax murderer and a park ranger.

Before You Judge Me

You might think you know where I'm coming from — a good Christian virginal bride, right? Sheltered — boring — so of course I'm going to try to frighten the bejeebies out of you and force you into my way of thinking. I'm going to try to steal your fun.

At the risk of giving you emotional whiplash,[10] I'm going to be brutally honest about my background. First though, I need to tell you about a conversation I had with my friend Rachel.

Meet Rachel

"So what about the fact that guys in the Bible treated women like sex slaves?" Rachel looked at me, level-eyed, smart, sassy. "The God of the Bible clearly doesn't put very much value on women."

---

10. You're going to learn that I have a tendency to jump from crazy stories to serious analogies.

It was obvious that Rachel viewed my waiting-to-have-sex-until-married plan as one that simply empowered men to take whatever they wanted when they wanted it after the knot was tied. And it was a *tight* knot.

My friend thought she had me. But what she didn't know was that hearing her question was somewhat like looking into a mirror. I'd asked the same question many times. I'll admit that at the time I asked that question, I was pretty jaded. Despite the fact I'd grown up in church — and even worse, was the pastor's kid[11] — I saw sex only inside of marriage as extremely constraining.

Why should married women have all the fun? Why did so many men seem to think it was their women's duties to fulfill their fantasies? Why should some man feel he had the *right* to my body?

Twenty-five percent of you — if statistics are true — have been exactly where I'm sitting right now.[8] To you, the thought of monogamous sex makes your stomach churn. You can't imagine giving one man that kind of leeway. Wouldn't it take away all *your* enjoyment? You want freedom rather than the long-term commitment of marriage, because quite frankly — like my friend and me — you can't imagine being with just one man.

The day Rachel confronted me, I came face-to-face with those thoughts and questions again. I struggled over the memory of one man who held me down, did unimaginable things to me, and threatened worse things if I told anyone. I was four years old. I believed him.

So you can imagine I had good reasons not to feel favorably about marriage. If that's how you're feeling, I want to share the words of my friend Madison with you. She speaks from a heart that experienced every way a man could take advantage of her[12] — until

---

11. You have no idea how hard that still is for me to admit.
12. The rest of her story is in chapter five.

she met the man she married, the one who cared more about her heart than her body.

Madison has this to say about sex inside of marriage:

> When you finally meet a guy who makes you feel like you are a princess, a priceless treasure, and he is honored just to get to be in your presence — when you meet that guy who listens to what you have to say and genuinely loves you for who you are as a person, not as a hot chick he can use for his personal pleasure; that guy who sees your worth and treasures it; that guy who goes out of his way to protect you even from himself — *then* you will realize that one guy you dated that one time (the one who made you cry) wasn't worth a single tear.

Ladies, that is God's guy for you. When you meet *that guy*, you're going to know it. He is going to be so caring and so compassionate and so in love with you that he is going to do anything for you. Even wait. And even let you experience sex without it being *his* power trip.

Don't believe me? Think guys like that don't exist?

I've been married to one for five years. So has Madison. So have over twenty of the other people who will share their stories in this book.

There are still days when I have to pinch myself. This woman — me, the one whose friends used to call her the "feminazi" — fell in love? This girl — me, the one who used to say, "singleness = happiness" and "marriage = bondage," gave her heart away? This woman — me, the one who said, "My husband died at birth," discovered he was actually very much alive and very much in love with her? And five years later this girl — me — is more free and more wrapped up in this man than she ever could have imagined?

See, this book is about finding — and waiting — for that man who will take your breath away. No matter how far you have or haven't gone sexually, I admire you for picking up this book. It takes courage to read the bare naked truth — it takes guts to acquaint yourself with a different perspective on sex — to get the facts from a new point of view.

So go ahead — dig down deep and take courage to believe there is a love deeper and more freeing than casual sex. I can't promise you a cookie if you'll crawl out from under the airplane seat, but I can promise you the truth. And I can promise you that the truth is what will set you free.

(UN)SCIENTIFIC QUIZ

Does Waiting Come Naturally to You?

1. When you want to buy something, you:
   a. Think about it awhile before you decide.
   b. Beg your parents for the money. (You already spent everything last week.)
   c. Wait for the urge to pass while counting your life savings.

2. Your boyfriend wants to make out. You:
   a. Give in for a few minutes.
   b. Actually, it was your idea.
   c. Tell him you're saving your first kiss for one year after you're married.

3. Your friends like you because:
   a. You're always willing to come along for the ride.
   b. You're the life of the party.
   c. You nag them about what their parents will say if they get caught in their sin.

4. Your biggest craving is:
   a. Some baked chips.
   b. A box of Ho Ho's.
   c. A carrot stick.

5. If you compared yourself to one celebrity, it would be:
   a. Selena Gomez
   b. Ke$ha
   c. Dakota Fanning

BARE NAKED RESULTS

Mostly a's: You're right in the middle, but this doesn't make you average. You've learned how to control your urges because you know it will benefit your life in the future. Keep up the good work.

Mostly b's: Whoa. Slow down. Life's a marathon, not a sprint. While waiting for the big things might not come naturally to you, it's something you can work on.

Mostly c's: You could probably afford to pick up the pace a little, although there's nothing wrong with being cautious. Just know that you don't have to be cautious out of fear. Let your hair down a little — your life will be richer for it.

BARE NAKED JOURNAL

What are some lies people commonly believe about sex?

_____

_____

_____

What are some lies you've believed about sex?

_____

_____

_____

Be honest: how open-minded are you feeling about learning some new truths?

_____

_____

Are you convinced the author of this book is insane, or are you going to give her a chance?

_____

_____

_____

LIE #2

Waiting Is for Wusses

THREE WORDS STRIKE FEAR in my heart faster than anything: *bathing suit season.*

Let me explain something: I was born pale.[1] When I go to the beach, young children scream and hide. "What is that?" they shout as they peer from behind the sand dunes.

I blame this public disgrace on my mother. No — not genetics. Sunscreen. I had no hope of achieving a flawless tan during my childhood. Mom was the founder of Sunscreen Addicts Anonymous. There wasn't a trip to the coast when she didn't slather me with cold, smelly cream. She was "protecting" my "beautiful" skin.

This led to my rebellion.

Some people do something drastic when they turn eighteen. They buy a pack of cigarettes or sneak into a nightclub.

---

1. Kind people call it "fair."

I went to the beach without sunscreen.

I was going to ignore the jeering and get a tan. I sat on Myrtle Beach for three days — sunscreenless. Nothing happened. I didn't even burn.

Then I saw it: a commercial stating that someone had invented the sunless tan.[2]

It was risky. None of my friends had tried it. I could think of a million reasons why it was a bad idea, but my heart kept telling me *I needed to stop being a wuss and get a tan.*

In the back of my mind, I didn't really believe I could try it. But that's how risk taking works. It starts as a simple contemplation. Once we let the contemplation on the porch, it bangs down the door. Before we know it, it's dragging us down the street through the front entrance of the tanning salon.

Kind of like the whole sex contemplation:

- Having sex is risky; not gonna do it (contemplation).
- But he's really cute (front porch).
- And he *likes* me (front door).
- And it *feels good* (dragging down the street).

Friends, we need to step away from the front porch altogether. Just like I should have done the morning I walked to the tanning salon.

The next thing I knew, an orange mist was spraying me in the face and goose bumps were running down my spine.

To say I was worried about my family's response would be an understatement. I'd kept my risk a secret — but now there was no turning back. I was orange. They would ask questions.[3]

I could create excuses. I'd been ill before. I could say I wasn't feeling well. That I'd eaten too many carrots.

---

2. Yes, I was alive when the sunless tan was invented. Stop snickering.
3. Just like you might think you can keep your sexual choices a secret. It might work for a while ... but eventually word's gonna get out.

Would I be cast out? Disowned? I could hear the sound of my own heartbeat as I walked up to the front porch and searched for my house key. Just my luck — I'd left it inside the house. I couldn't even sneak in and wash away the evidence.

I reached for the doorbell with shaky hands. The door opened, and my petite mother stood staring at me. Her mouth gaped. She stood wordless for a moment — in shock. Finally, she stuttered.

"Phil … Phil … Philip … come … come see your sister!"

My brother wandered to the front door and stopped suddenly. There I stood — as orange as the morning sunrise. He tried to contain himself. He tried with everything that was inside of him. But he couldn't.

His face turned beet red. Then he started to … laugh in a way I'd never heard before.

"I know — I know it's bad," I said. I stared at the concrete in shame. "It'll get better … I think … it should fade …"

It did get better. Just in time for Easter morning, the tan faded into a mellow brown. For the first time in my life, I wore a sundress.[4] Everyone asked if I'd been to the beach. I smiled. I had my tan.

Then something horrible happened. Something unimaginable. Something unthinkable. The tan began to peel, piece by piece. My friends watched amazedly. My enemies laughed hysterically. My family smiled sympathetically. Sort of.

How could I let this happen? I wondered. *How could I have been so stupid?*

The truth is, it happened because I'm a risk taker.[5] Sometimes I've taken good risks. Sometimes I've taken bad risks. I'm starting to learn the difference, but I'm a slow learner.

That's exactly why seven years ago I made another risky decision —

---

4. It was my sister's.
5. Aka idiot.

this time for my benefit — when I decided to do something I knew might bring me shame. I decided to wait for the right guy to have sex with. I decided I wanted that guy to be committed to me. I decided I wanted that guy to be my husband.

I can still remember sitting there arguing with myself about it. Knowing the ridicule that would come was way worse than the long-lasting aftereffects of any spray-on tan.

> **BaRe NaKeD tip**
>
> Think things through beforehand. Don't decide in the heat of the moment.

To wait or not to wait? That was the question.

I'd heard people talk about "purity" and "saving yourself." But to be honest, it all sounded a little lame to me. What if I really loved someone? Waiting seemed like a wussy thing to do. Wasn't the risk of getting caught — the risk of something unexpected happening — half the thrill of having sex?

But what if I was fooling myself? What if the truly risky thing was having the guts to believe that someone out there was the one for me physically — and emotionally? What if the truly risky thing was finding the strength to ignore the ridicule of my friends? What if the truly risky thing was saying no even when my body was shouting, "Yes! Yes! *Yes!*"?

I knew in my heart … I wanted to wait. The rewards were worth it. I wanted to share this experience — this opening of my entire self — with not just someone I met in high school. I wanted to share it with someone who loved not only my body but also my heart.

> **Forty-six percent of you are virgins.[a] Virginity is not what I mean by "waiting," because you can start waiting anytime regardless of the past.**

I wish I could say that was it — that I decided and my purity plans were all taken care of. That I never thought about it again. But I was a red-blooded girl. I noticed guys. I noticed how they looked, how they smelled, and how their skin felt when they brushed against me. I noticed how they eyed me. I noticed how chill bumps ran down my spine.

My friend Erynn noticed these things too. And even though she wasn't a wuss, she didn't really want to tell her boyfriend about her decision to wait. Which resulted in an … umm … interesting relationship to say the least.

SPOTLIGHT
Author Erynn Mangum

When I was a sophomore or junior in high school, I decided that I wanted my first kiss to be when I got engaged. I thought it would be so romantic[6] and I also thought it would protect me from kissing a bunch of guys that I would inevitably end up not marrying. Both good reasons. Both things my new boyfriend did not know.

We were standing on the porch, and it was a little bit chilly since it was early April. It was also completely dark outside except for the porch lights and the stars, and Jon bent down and …

I realized what he was about to do right before he kissed me, so I instinctively turned my head, and he ended up kissing my cheek.

It was *so* awkward!

And then I was so completely flustered that all I could say was, "Okay, well, good night. Drive carefully!" and then hurry inside and close the door.

Poor Jon. I was so rattled when I got inside. I walked into the

---

6. Note from Bekah: Erynn writes romantic stuff, but decided to wait to kiss. Read her books to see if her characters feel the same way.

kitchen, and both my mom and dad were in there. Dad asked what had happened, because it was obvious that *something* had.

I told them that Jon had tried to kiss me and I'd turned my head, and they both started laughing so hard. Dad said, "Well. That is probably the last we'll see of him."

Not only did Jon call the next day (so glad Dad was wrong!), but he also came over for dinner. And the entire time he was there, I kept trying to tell him about my no-kissing stance, but each time I opened my mouth, someone would walk into the room, or dinner was ready, or the movie was starting.

So, once again, I went the whole night without saying anything, and it was again time for the awkward porch good-night thing. This time though, he hugged me and stepped back. "Well, good night," he said.

I almost just let him leave. Then I felt bad about the previous night again and mustered up my nerve. "Jon, I just want you to know that I'm saving my first kiss for when I get engaged, so I'm sorry I didn't tell you, but it was kind of weird last night, and also, by the way, I don't date casually, and I'm sorry, and anyways, good night," I said, all in one breath, and then I ran for the door.

He left, and I closed the door and took a deep breath.

Then the doorbell rang again.

And it was Jon — who calmly announced that we needed to talk more about this and asked if I could join him on the porch for a little bit. I sat down on the bench out front, fully expecting him to say that my romantic ideal wasn't going to fly with him, so I was either going to need to pucker up or plan on him leaving. So I planned on him leaving. Because being with someone who didn't respect my boundaries — regardless of how pointless, silly, or stupid he thought they were — just wasn't an option.

He sat down next to me, and we ended up talking for the next two hours about me and why I wasn't going to kiss anyone and the whole not casually dating thing, and why that was okay with him. And then he said, "Look, Erynn, I wouldn't be here if I didn't think there was a possibility of marrying you someday."

Um. Okay.

Then we said good-bye (again), and he left (again), and I walked back into the house (again). I'm pretty sure my parents thought we were ending it outside and that it was probably the shortest relationship ever, next to Britney Spears's fifty-five-hour Vegas marriage, but, happily, they were wrong.[7]

* * *

Sometimes I wish I'd known Erynn when she decided to wait.[8] Sometimes in high school I thought I was the only person on earth taking this risk. Sometimes I wondered if any guy would want someone as inexperienced as I was. Sometimes I thought I would end up a forty-year-old virgin.[9] So I did stupid stuff to comfort myself. Stuff like create mental lists like this:

Celebrities Who Say They Believe in Abstinence

- Jordin Sparks (*American Idol*): "My parents gave me a purity ring and talked to me about waiting until I'm married to have sex. It wasn't forced; it just made perfect sense. It's going to be awesome to say to my husband that I waited my whole life for him."[b] "It's hard every day, but I made a promise to myself. Temptation is always there. It's all about making the right choice and not putting yourself in that situation."[c]

- Lolo Jones (Olympic hurdler and bobsledder): She says saving herself for her husband has been harder than training for two Summer Games.[d]

---

7. Erynn has been married to Jon for several years now — happily, I might add. And since they have a kid, I'm going to assume they got the whole kissing, etc., thing down.
8. Some of you are shouting, "Yes!"
9. You can stop mocking now.

You may have noticed this list is a little on the short side.[10] I told myself that it was because if waiting was easy, everybody would be doing it. *If waiting wasn't a risk*, I thought, *more people would be risking their reputations to do it.* The truth is, Hollywood isn't exactly the best representation of the general public.

Some people in Hollywood[11] would have us believe:

- Sleeping around is healthy exploration of our sexuality.
- Our own happiness is what matters.
- We weren't made to be monogamous.
- We will eventually find the person who completes us.

God wants us to believe:

- Healthy exploration of our sexuality happens with our life-time soul mates (Hebrews 13:4).
- Our happiness is intertwined with the happiness of our soul mates (1 Corinthians 7:3 – 5).
- God made us to be one-man women (1 Corinthians 7:2).
- We are complete in God; our relationships with others reflect that (Philippians 2:2).

It may not feel like it every day, but there are people out there who have taken the risk of waiting. They're probably not talking about it over lunch, but they do exist. People like my friend Jan, who

BARE NAKED QUOTE

"Waiting isn't for wusses. But waiting is for people who have discovered how valuable their hearts are, and who are not willing to let them go for anything less than they deserve."

– *Author Denise Hildreth Jones*

---

10. Which didn't exactly inspire my confidence.
11. No names included, as I prefer not to get sued.

had a moment when she also realized that maybe waiting isn't the wussiest thing.

SPOTLIGHT
Author Jan Kern

Okay, picture this: there was a school event at the *other* high school, and my friend who attended there had this guy she wanted me to meet. I liked her and trusted her, so the guy should be cool, right? I met him, and yep, he was cool. Tall, brown hair, blue eyes, a football player. He got me with the first look at his perfectly straight teeth. Like that's supposed to tell me a lot?

I don't know what it took for him, but he asked me out, and soon I was wearing his class ring. I know — back in the day, right? I was a little shy at the time, so I was kinda glad he was at the other school. I felt nervous most of the time I was around him.

That should have been a sign.

My parents were newly divorced. My dad lived in another state, and I lived with my mom. She was wonderful in countless ways but also hurting and too busy trying to survive to be entirely on top of what I was out doing. In other words, there wasn't much guidance going on, and I wasn't asking.

One night after going to a movie, Cool Football Player wanted me to meet a few of his friends. I felt that warning twinge of nerves but didn't say anything. We drove from party to party, and I began to gather a few new facts about Football Player. He drank. A lot. And he liked to get close to me. Very close.

I was new in my faith, but I felt a clear conflict inside. I really had grown to care about this guy, and he had captured a piece of my heart. Still, I knew it was time to end the game. With genuine tears, I unwrapped the fuzzy yarn I'd used to resize his ring and gave that ring back. I told him I really cared about him, but we had different priorities. I'd say that was the century's understatement. I did try to share my new faith with him. He wasn't interested.

But it ended well. Really, it did. He respected me, and even over the years when I would run into him in different places, I still felt that respect from him. I don't think I would have had that if I had not ended our relationship when I did. More important, I would have lost respect for myself.

I entirely credit God. I was new at living out my Christian life, but He protected me from going further into a relationship that could have gone very wrong. I wasn't taught to think prayerfully or carefully, to look at a situation from multiple angles, to listen to those alerts within, but He showed me how. Talking things over with Him became a vital lifeline for me. He also brought mentors into my life who helped me consider all the angles of my choices, especially in honoring Him, honoring myself, and honoring others.

I tried it. It worked. I discovered that thinking things through and having that voice to say yes to the right things and no to the destructive ones wasn't constricting. It was amazing and utterly freeing.

* * *

That's how I kept taking the risk of waiting — by surrounding myself with people like Jan. People who didn't talk about sex twenty-four/seven. Some of them were virgins. Some weren't. Some of them will share their stories in this book — both the ones who waited and the ones who decided it wasn't worth the wait.

Me? I kept taking the risk. The risk that maybe, just maybe, someone was out there saving his heart for me instead of giving it away to twenty other girls.

On August 4, 2007, the payoff of that risk — a curly-haired, broad-shouldered guy — looked me in the eyes and pledged forever

> ### BARE NAKED QUOTE
>
> "I'll be honest, I think one of the best parts about waiting for my man is that I never think of anyone else. Never. I don't have anyone to compare him to. He's my best."
>
> — *Author Lynn Martin Cowell*

to me. He promised to love, cherish, and shelter me. He promised to be faithful to me, and because he had chosen to be faithful to me long before we even met, I knew he meant to keep that promise.

Two hours after the wedding ceremony, we said good-bye to our friends and made out like we'd never made out before. Things were on a steady roll when we made it to our hotel, only to discover ...

The wait wasn't over.

Apparently, hotels expect some sort of monetary transaction before they'll give you a room. We knew this beforehand, but I'd cleaned out my bank account in order to buy Ethan's wedding band. It was then we discovered that ... my new husband had accidentally left his bank card in the ATM early that morning. We had no money and no way to finish what we'd started.[12]

As we fished out an old credit card, it dawned on us that anyone could be spending our meager honeymoon savings from his card. We headed straight to our honeymoon suite ... to call the credit card company.[13]

To say our first half hour as an officially married couple was awkward would be an understatement. I lay draped across the couch while Ethan argued on the phone with three bank employees, all asking questions in foreign accents. ("What color is the card? Please hold ...")

---

12. Unless you count the backseat of Ethan's pickup, which was likely to get us arrested.
13. Romantic, I know.

Those thirty minutes pretty much surmised our entire journey to that point. The wait was inexpressibly difficult … but totally worth it.

So to all the girls out there who are tempted to believe that maybe, just maybe, waiting isn't for wusses and that waiting is worth the risk, I'm here to say this is the bare naked truth: *When you find the right guy, he will be worth all the risk taking and waiting in the world.*

(UN)SCIENTIFIC QUIZ

Are You a Risk Taker?

1. When you're at the amusement park, you:
   a. Take a seat on the Ferris wheel.
   b. Head straight for the fifty-foot death drop.
   c. Go to the kiddie coasters and grab on for dear life.

2. In a crowded room at a party, you:
   a. Stand on the edge and make small talk.
   b. Walk into the center of the room and start telling jokes.
   c. Close your eyes and hope it will all go away.

3. You crash your parents' car. The first thing you do is:
   a. See if there's a way you can cover the scratch.
   b. Scratch? The thing is totaled because you were going 100 mph.
   c. What car? The sidewalk is more your style.

4. You've been asked to give a speech, so you:
   a. Plan the craziest story-telling, attention-grabbing moment ever.
   b. Go bungee jumping for joy.
   c. Pretend to have an exotic fever that day, complete with fake purple lesions.

5. Your friend says you'd look great with pink hair. You:
   a. Think about it for a few days, then go to the salon.
   b. Think it's the best idea you've ever had. Why not try it at home — now?
   c. Decide to go with chestnut brown instead.

BARE NAKED RESULTS

Mostly a's: You think about risks before you take them, but you're not afraid to have fun. You have great balance, and your life is exciting because of it. Here's hoping you use the same process when it comes to weighing the risks that come with waiting!

Mostly b's: Your spontaneity makes you a lot of fun to be around. You like to live life on the edge. This is okay sometimes, but it might be a good idea to think through your impulses before making an important decision. Like, you know, the one we've been talking about in this book.

Mostly c's: You run from big risks, but that isn't necessarily a bad thing. You think before you act, and that can work to your advantage especially when it comes to the virginity issue. Still, don't be afraid to try new things and think outside the box when a situation might call for it — you might find out you like being an occasional risk taker!

BARE NAKED JOURNAL

What's the biggest risk you've ever taken? How did it work out for you?

_____

_____

_____

Be honest. Is your fear of never finding _him_ keeping you from making the decision to wait?

_____

_____

_____

LIE #3

Guys Won't Want Me If I'm Not Experienced

THE OFFICE HAS PLYWOOD walls, oil-stained carpet, and grease thicker than a corpse's makeup. There is one purpose to this place: function.

Men come here every day to design and build things. From a woman's perspective, though, the walls need to be painted, the carpet needs to be replaced, and the HAZMAT team needs to be summoned ASAP.

There is one office item in pristine condition, though: the Budweiser Girl. She is tacked up squarely without a wrinkle or a stain.[1] I am not the Budweiser Girl. In fact, looking at that bronzed, flat-abbed model makes me want to do something drastic — like

---

1. Clearly the guys who work here have their priorities straight.

draw stretch marks on her perfectly shaped boobs.

I'm not gonna lie. Places like this office make me wonder about men. Are all guys obsessed with perfect girls? If sex is the *one* thing that seems to matter to them, shouldn't a girl be amazing — in every way? Even in experience?

BaRe NaKeD tip

Only compare yourself to others when you can win.

This got me thinking. I decided that if I wanted to know more than just my guy's opinion, I would have to ask other guys about perfect sex. So I confronted them face-to-face.

Actually, I chickened out. Because it would be really awkward to confront boys about how perfect they want their girls to be.[2] So I Facebooked them instead. And I was surprised at how many of them responded.

"When/if you get/got married, how 'experienced' did/do you want your girl to be?" I asked. (Some of these guys were already married, some of them were dating, and some weren't even in a relationship.) Here's what several of them said:

> "Guys want girls to know how to do everything without ever having done anything. At all. To or with anyone." — Brad

This made me laugh. Out loud. It sounded a little extreme. But John, twenty-one and currently engaged, responded this way:

> "I actually love the idea of both of us being 'beginners' together. It means a lot to me to know that she waited for me and we can both gain experience together."

And Derek, who has dated both "experienced" and "inexperienced" girls, answered this way:

---

2. "So um … how's your sex life?"

"I think it's [more difficult] for a guy (at least it was for me) to be with a girl who is 'experienced,' because we're afraid that we won't live up to her past experiences — that we won't be as memorable as the guys she's been with before."

I started to notice a theme: There *are* guys out there who are waiting for sex, or even if they haven't waited, are starting to appreciate waiting now. They — possibly like you — have recognized the value, physically and emotionally, of not sleeping with ten other people before marriage. They want the bond with their spouses to be strong — they want to experience the emotional and psychological benefits I mentioned in chapter one of hanging in there for the right person.

Like Michael, who just got married three weeks ago. He had this to say about having a girl who decided to wait for him:

There is a popular idea that says a woman cares primarily about the emotional, while guys just care about the physical. Maybe this is where some girls get the idea that experience is better; if they are experienced, then they can better please a guy. There is some truth to the above dichotomy, but it is often severely overstated. Guys also care a lot about the emotional aspects of sex and relationships; the supposed "benefits" of experience don't outweigh the emotional baggage attached. For whatever reason, our culture today equates manliness with lack of emotion. Guys want to live up to this expectation and therefore shroud their emotions.

The idea that inexperience is shameful is completely crazy. No guy whose mind has not been completely warped would [think inexperience is a bad thing]. I am tremendously grateful that when I am with my wife … I can look into her eyes without any suspicion that she is comparing me to, or thinking about, another incident or guy. There is a lot of freedom and joy in that, probably more than I know, having never experienced it otherwise.

Like so many girls, my friend Tabetha says she wishes she'd known there were guys like this out there — guys who weren't boring but were willing to wait for the right girl.

SPOTLIGHT
Tabetha Brown

Was it love? No (now that I look back at it), but it was love that I was searching for, love that I craved, love that I never saw at home.

See, my mom started singing in a Christian band when I was seven. She was gone almost every weekend. Sometimes we went with her to gigs, but it got to the point where my dad stopped going, and so did we. My mother ended up having an "emotional" affair with one of the singers in the band, which later resulted in my parents' divorce. When my parents split, I tried to find that missing love in other places. I was a virgin for the longest time, until I met a boy who said all the "right" things. It was the day before I turned nineteen.

After that boy and I had sex, I felt so trapped. I started to believe a lie: I had to exchange sex if I wanted love. This boy and I stayed together for about two years. It was a horrible relationship that scarred me emotionally.

I wish I could say that my "first" was my last until I got married. He wasn't. I found myself in more bad relationships where sex was expected. I felt guilty about it, but it became easier each time. It's ironic that every relationship where I gave myself away ended up falling apart.

I finally cried out to God. He answered and showed me that His love was enough. When I gave my life to Him, I promised to abstain from sex until I was married. I started to read the Bible, go to church, and focus on the plans He had for me. I finally felt peace. But everything wasn't suddenly perfect: Even though I continued to date, the fact that I would not have sex drove most men away.

The next year, I met David on a blind date. He was different — passionate about music and the Lord. God had answered my prayer in the instant I met this guy.

As David and I began to get to know each other, I found out that he hadn't dated anyone in about three and a half years. (My friends said something must be wrong with him.) Because he had some bad relationships in the past, David had chosen to give his dating life to God. I was excited to find out that my boyfriend was a virgin but was immediately brokenhearted because I had not waited for him.

When I told David I wasn't a virgin, we had a long talk about my past and the issues my sex life had created. Because of the choices I'd made, I was insecure about my body. David actually started working on these issues with me and still works with me on them today.

Once I'd met "the one," not having sex wasn't easy. I missed the feeling of intimacy that comes with sex and wanted to experience that with David. I knew it would be so much different with him. But when we agreed to wait, it opened up a whole new world of romance.

David proposed nine months after we met. I had been proposed to in the past, but not like this. He actually took time to make everything personal and special. We're both so glad we spent time focusing on our relationship before we began to focus on the physical.

It's been two years since we got married, and I'm now pregnant with our first child. I'm looking forward to telling our son about the freedom that comes through waiting for his future wife — whether she has waited for him or not.

* * *

God Wants You — Experienced or Inexperienced

For me to end the chapter here would be an injustice, because I'd only be telling half the story. Maybe, like Tabetha, you've already given yourself away. Your heart is racing with emotions right now because you've already lived the regret she so openly talks about. Maybe it was only once — or maybe it was over and over and over. You hoped to feel love in exchange for your sexuality, but in the end you only felt emptiness. That's a high cost for a low return.

I'm reminded of one of my favorite people. If you're familiar with the Bible at all, you probably know the fictional story Jesus told about the prodigal son. (If you don't know the story, and have a moment and a Bible, flip to Luke 15:11 – 32.) In a moment of rash decision, the son left his father and spent his entire inheritance on things he thought would satisfy his emptiness. It seemed this guy had it all — a sudden group of friends and all the money he could want. But when the money was gone, so were his friends.

You probably know where I'm going with this. Someone used you. Like the prodigal son's friends, they took what they wanted. You thought that giving yourself to this someone would make you feel loved, but it didn't. And the question was left mingling with your fears: *Am I not enough?*

You are enough.

Can I say that again?

You are enough.

My friend John says that Satan layers lies on top of pain. When someone abandons you after they take what they want, Satan's lie to you is that you are not enough. And as soon as you begin to believe that lie, you do one of two things: You hunker down and promise never to trust anyone with your heart again, or you go on to the next person and silently try to prove to yourself *I am enough.*

Both of these actions are dangerous because they are based on lies. But the second action, moving on to the next guy, is the more dangerous of the two because it creates what I call a cycle of regret.

Now, I'm not trying to say what my friend Abbie says most of her youth leaders told her growing up: "Boys are testosterone-driven dogs, and girls are sluts." No. I'm just saying that it's human nature to take what you want and then leave. The truth is not that you are lacking something. The truth is that the guy who takes what he wants from you is actually stuck in his own cycle of regret. It might look something like this:

Cycle of Regret

He leaves you

You give yourself away

He takes what he wants

As nice as it sounds, there really isn't such a thing as "friends with benefits." As I mentioned in chapter one, sex creates physiological ties. And with those ties come feelings.

It is impossible to have a physical act without an emotional consequence. It's simply a law: every action has a reaction.

A Guy's Cycle of Regret

He leaves you

He takes what he wants

He feels guilty

And for a guy, the reaction to developing an emotional tie to you before he's ready is that, often, he will run.

This is why you don't want to date a guy who has a reputation for sleeping around. You might think it isn't going to happen to

> ## BARE NAKED QUOTE
>
> "You may be sorry for *not* waiting, but you'll never be sorry for waiting."
>
> *— Author Marla DeShong Alupoaicei*

you — that he treats you differently, that you are the one who can finally satisfy him. *But, honey, it ain't about you.* It doesn't matter how amazing or experienced you are in bed, *he is eventually going to leave you.* You might be able to keep his interest for longer than the other girls, but eventually he's going to develop feelings for you. And when that happens, he's going to run like crazy.

Now I know the running thing might seem counterintuitive. After all, when *you* develop feelings for a guy, it makes you want to move closer to him — not hightail it away. But boys are different. They mature at a different pace.[3] So while you're thinking *stability, forever love,* and *my one and only,* he's thinking, *What?! I just wanted to have sex!*[4]

And when that happens, you're going to find yourself at the beginning of the cycle of regret. Eventually, you'll go through the rotation often enough that, like Tabetha, the pain will numb to a dull ache. But really, is that how you want to go through life? Numb? Unable to give or receive true love in a future marriage?

I'm saying some pretty strong things here, but it's because I want you to know my heart for you. Your enemy will tell you anything you want to hear, but a true friend will tell you what you need to hear, even when it hurts (see Proverbs 27:6).

It's time to break the cycle of regret that leads to numbness. But if we're going to break it, we have to drastically make changes to our perspective. Changes like Shannon encouraged her friend to make.

---

3. I don't mean that as a slam. Really.
4. Can you blame him? You're really hot.

SPOTLIGHT
Author Shannon Primicerio

I was in junior high the first time my friend told me she was gaining sexual experience so she would "have an awesome wedding night." When I asked for more info, she said, "How will sex ever be any fun when I'm married if I don't know what I'm doing?"

I stammered awkwardly, and we moved on. But I never forgot that conversation. Years later, when I was in college, I was cleaning my dorm room one night when another friend began talking about the same thing. In the process of our conversation, I sliced my arm open on the edge of my dresser while she chatted away about "things that aren't sex but give you sexual experience."

"Hey," I interrupted her. "You don't happen to have a Band-Aid, do you?" I pressed a tissue to my arm and sat down next to her on the futon.

"No," she said, "only this one." She held up her hand to show a bloody Band-Aid wrapped around her index finger. Disgusted, I declined her offer. And then it hit me.

"Here's what's wrong with the reasoning that a guy is going to want a sexually experienced wife," I began as my mind raced. "A guy might want sex from a girl now, but he's certainly not going to want a wife who was used by every other guy she met." My friend looked at me, curious.

"When I sliced my arm open," I went on, "I didn't want a used Band-Aid. I wasn't looking for an *experienced* Band-Aid. Instead, I was looking for a new Band-Aid. I didn't want a Band-Aid used by everyone. I wanted a Band-Aid just for me."

Slowly, a look of understanding crossed my friend's face, and she nodded. While a guy might want a girl for sex now, a real man who will want her for who she is will want all of her just for himself. He won't want a girl with every other guy's fingerprints all over her. Suddenly the concept of being sexually experienced seemed less appealing.

But what if I already have some sexual experience, you may be wondering. *Is it too late for me? Should I let guys keep using me since a real man might never want me?*

No! This is where God's grace has an opportunity to enter your life in a big way. Psalm 51:7 says, "Wash me, and I will be whiter than snow." Ask God to forgive you, and resolve to live differently. Choose to embrace a secondary purity that will allow you to save the rest of yourself for a real man who is worth it.

If there's one thing it is always okay to be experienced in, it's walking in God's grace.

* * *

Lighten Up: How Choosing Teams Breaks the Cycle of Regret

I'm gonna be honest here: I'm pretty sure I'm the reason they put warnings on athletic equipment. In my first[5] year on a soccer team, I was the only person who ever won the Most Frequently Injured Award.

I ruined a lot of people's bets by even making it to the end of the season. After the first game (when I was knocked upside the head by the soccer ball) and the second game (when I ate grass like a dairy cow), there were some doubts.[6] Even in my own mind. But in the end I knew: I had made a commitment, and I needed to keep it. (Stop snickering — the fact that food was served between halves had nothing to do with my decision.)

Okay, I confess. I wasn't really a committed player. I only scored

---

5. And only.
6. And *hopes* that I would quit.

one goal that season. But I'll never forget that moment. I'll always remember the exhilaration that flooded my soul as the beautiful black and white ball soared to the back of the net — and stayed there. The team cheered loudly.

The *other* team, that is.

"What were you thinking?" my coach screamed. "You just scored for the opposing team!"

As I dug my hole to China, I realized I'd lost my focus. All I heard was the crowd screaming, "Run! Run! Run!" So I had run. In the completely wrong direction. And I had scored. For the completely wrong team.[7]

Maybe you're asking how I could be enough of an idiot to forget which team was mine.[8] Maybe you've never forgotten which team was yours. Or maybe — just maybe — you have.

Your life is a lot like that soccer game. There are teams, but sometimes it's unclear which side you should be playing on. See, God is not making rules about sex just to make you miserable. He is making them because he wants you to score big within his design of marriage — but you can't have it both ways. You're scoring for one team, or you're scoring for the other.

Which team are you on?

A lot of girls are walking around church today claiming to be on God's team while acting like they're not. Is that you? And if it is, are you ready to switch sides?

But What about My Past?

If it was as easy as *just deciding* in your head to switch teams, more people would be successful in choosing to wait. But when you're stuck in a cycle of regret, it's going to take more than that initial

---

7. Yes, this is a true story.
8. Years later, I'm still asking that.

intellectual decision (but the decision is crucial). Eventually your heart is going to start asking "Am I enough?" again. You're going to be tempted to run into the arms of a boy to answer that question.

Here's the key: Run somewhere else. Run to the creator of the universe, to the romancer of your soul.

So I want you to ask the question. No, really, I mean it. Right now. Put down this book, close your eyes, and ask God, "Am I enough?"

You picked the book right up again, didn't you? I'm serious. Put it back down. And don't just ask the question this time — wait for an answer. Close your eyes and wait for God to respond. I'm not saying to wait for thunderclouds. I'm just saying to wait for a picture or a verse or a song or a promise to come to mind — something from God's heart to yours. If you know Him as your Savior, His Holy Spirit lives inside of you and He's waiting to talk to you.

He says, "Call to me and I will answer you and tell you great and unsearchable things you do not know" (Jeremiah 33:3).

Wait.

Wait.

Wait for it.

'Kay.

Now write down what God said. I mean it. You probably don't think you'll forget it right now, but later on when your heart is badgering you with the question of "Am I enough?" and you feel yourself being sucked into that cycle of regret, you need to remember what God said to you today and run home.

What This Means for Your Current Relationship

The way I see it, you're in one of two relationships right now.

1. You might be dating Mr. Fabulous. You have your moments when you're both tempted to take things too far. But he

doesn't constantly pressure you for sex. If this is the case, it's not wrong to hang in there with your relationship. (I would encourage you, however, not to go too deep emotionally.)[9]

Break the cycle before it's too late.

2. You might be dating Mr. Insistent. Your handsome prince just won't get off the sex topic. Yet God has talked to you today and told you that you're his. That you are enough without your guy. That you don't need sexual experience to be worth something to someone. That you are already worth the world to him and to your future spouse.

So if you fall into Category Two, how do you know what to do with your unhealthy relationship? Is it really unhealthy if you feel so drawn to him?

I recently asked my friend Madison these very questions. I knew she'd been stuck in the cycle of regret before she met her husband, and I knew she'd successfully broken that cycle. She responded with the following letter to her sixteen-year-old self.

DEAR SIXTEEN-YEAR-OLD ME

The worst thing you could do is settle for someone who tears you down. Someone who makes you feel like you have to do something to keep him. Someone who manipulates you in any way, shape, or form. That guy is not worth your tears, your guilt, or your shame.

---

9. Several of my friends are happily married to their high-school sweethearts. And most of them chose to limit how they spent time together in high school, setting up emotional boundaries that led to their current success.

You should not have to do *anything* to keep a guy. And if he makes you feel like you're going to lose him if you don't give him your body, then *good riddance*!

Sixteen-year-old me: When you begin to notice a pattern in the guys you date (a bad one), do yourself a favor. Sit down and assess what it is about them that draws you to them. Write out the reasons you realize they were unhealthy relationships, as well as a list of things you honestly want in the man you marry.

Ask your mature friends what they see in the guys you have dated in the past. And the next time you start dating someone, be friends with them first before you jump into the romantic side of things. If he is unwilling to be around your friends or family, it's a pretty big red flag.

How does he treat his family? Is he kind and respectful? Does he become a different person? Does he try to separate you from your family or friends? These are all things to pay attention to.

On the flip side, if he is kind, respectful of others (particularly women), listens to your opinions, doesn't make crude jokes or talk about sexual things around you, is patient and respects your boundaries (or even better, sets up boundaries himself to protect you), has a good relationship with his family and yours, looks your dad and brothers in the eye — these are all *great* signs.

One stellar test of his intentions is to invite him to church with you and your family. See how he responds.

Sixteen-year-old me, your body is *your* body. *No one else's.* It is not for anyone else's use. If at any point you feel like you *have* to do something physical (even just a hug) to keep a boy, then he is *not* a good choice. *Run* in the opposite direction. But when you meet the guy who, with his words and his actions, makes you feel like a princess, he is worth a second look.

Love,
Twenty-nine-year-old me

* * *

When You Need to Break It Off

Bekah here. So you need to tell a guy it isn't going to work. Easy, right? If you're laughing, you know what I'm talking about. It's never easy to break someone's heart. And let's face it: that's what you're essentially going to do. But ya know something? He's going to appreciate it. No — I mean it. He might not appreciate it at the moment. In fact, you're probably going to feel like the villain when you do it. But in the end, this guy is going to appreciate your honesty so he can move on.

Setting the Scene

When you break it off with a guy depends on the guy and the circumstances of your relationship. One thing is certain, though: When you break it off, you need to mean it. And if you're gonna mean it, you need to start by confessing to God that the relationship is wrong.

Yes, I said "confessing."

I know that's not a popular word. But if you have been going too far with your boyfriend, just saying you aren't going to do it anymore isn't going to work. You need to recognize it as sin and turn away from that sin — offering God nothing less than a clean break.

After you've told God you're done with this sin in your life, He promises He'll forgive you and give you strength to do what's right (1 John 1:9). Remember the story of the prodigal son? What I didn't tell you is that he went home. He was empty and broken and lost, but he knew enough to go home. And when he went home, this is what Jesus said happened: "While he was still a long way off, his father saw him and was filled with compassion for him; he ran to his son, threw his arms around him and kissed him" (Luke 15:20).

God wants you to come home. He is waiting for you with open arms. His dreams are so much bigger for you than the heartaches you're living in. He wants to help you break your cycle of regret. So here are some tips to help you end an unhealthy relationship.

There doesn't need to be a lot of drama, but you do need to be firm with this guy. None of this break-up/get back-together stuff.[10] If a guy is pressuring you to become more experienced in bed, there is no wavering here. If he's treating you, like Madison said, as anything less than a princess, it's time to end it — no matter how he promises to change. (And time to read chapter eight on why *you don't need him*.) So where should this breakup take place? Let's hear from Madison, the self-proclaimed queen of breakups (before she got off the cycle of regrets):

> If the guy you're breaking up with has shown himself to be violent or prone to outbursts, then make sure you talk to him about it in a public place, or even better bring along people who could protect you. The important thing is to be honest and just tell him that you realize things aren't working out and it's over. It sounds harsh, but the reality is that it is better to sever the relationship as quickly as possible. The longer you drag it out, the harder and often more painful it can become.

So now you have got your battle plan. You're armed. You're ready. And you know that you are prepared, with God's help, to start a new cycle. It looks like this:

God does have someone amazing out there for you. If you really want to know who that person is, he isn't the guy

Brand-New Cycle

He reaffirms you and meets your needs

You wonder if you're enough

You run to Jesus

---

10. Seriously — stay home from school and watch soap operas if you're craving theater.

who tacked up the Budweiser Girl poster. So go ahead — do what you've wanted to do all along. Join me in tearing down that image from that wall of your mind. And when we're done, we'll draw some stretch marks on her boobs. Just for good measure.

And then, also for good measure:

(UN)SCIENTIFIC QUIZ

Are You Attracted to "Bad Boys"?

1. Chris wants you to sneak out to meet him. You:
   a. Tell him to get lost. But your heart's pounding at the idea …
   b. Where? What time?
   c. Tell him you'll think about it, but plan to stay put, thanks.

2. Your mom hates your edgy guy. You:
   a. Break up. In person. He should know you mean business.
   b. Scream at her about how misunderstood you are.
   c. Roll your eyes but break up with him anyway.

3. He's coming onto you for sex. You:
   a. Slap his hand. And his face. Just for good measure.
   b. Go for it. You only live once.
   c. Back away … a little more slowly than your mind's telling you to.

4. Your friends tell you he's bad news. You:
   a. Tell him exactly what they said and ask for the truth.
   b. Ignore their warnings — he's the most fun you've ever had.
   c. Stop and look for evidence that he might be using you.

5. He tells you sex is okay because he loves you. You:
   a. Stop, drop, and roll your way out of the car.
   b. Give it a minute more of playful flirting.
   c. Make a mental note never to go out with him again. Or anyone else remotely like him.

BARE NAKED RESULTS

Mostly a's: You're sometimes attracted to "bad boys," but you keep a good head on your shoulders. You put yourself first, and that's the most important thing. Good work!

Mostly b's: You crave excitement, but you're expressing it in potentially dangerous ways. It might be time to reach out for some answers as to why you get a thrill out of living on the edge.

Mostly c's: You definitely crave the good guys. You're not in much danger of falling for the wrong person!

BARE NAKED JOURNAL

What do you think most guys want in a girl?

_____

_____

_____

What do you think you want in your future spouse?

_____

_____

_____

What are some sacrifices you've made in the past to feel loved?

_____

_____

_____

What's your battle plan for breaking an unhealthy relationship if you're in one?

_____

_____

_____

LIE #4

Sex Is Okay as Long as It's Safe

No one likes the word *accident*. No one plans on it. When was the last time you heard someone say, "I think I'll have an accident tomorrow. What do you think, Howard? Is tomorrow a good day for a tragedy?"

"By golly, Marge, I think tomorrow is a great day for a tragedy. What time should we plan for?"

Tragedy strikes us out of nowhere. I know what it's like to be struck out of nowhere. It happened to me a few years ago.[1] I was minding my own business, cleaning out my car, when — *wham!* — all of a sudden my vacuum cleaner stopped working. That was tragedy number one.

---

1. 1. I was still living with the parents.

Tragedy number two happened when my vacuum cleaner not only stopped working, it started barfing. The barfing actually began with the burping.[2]

Oh, that's cute, I thought. *The vacuum has indigestion.*

Two seconds later, indigestion turned into burping, which turned into hurling, which turned into a disgusting mess on the backseat of my car.

But I couldn't give up. Not now. Not when I was so close to finding out the original color of my upholstery.

My mind reeled for a solution.

Replace the bag? No, too much work.

Call the CDC? A strong possibility.

Borrow the neighbor's vacuum?

Woot! I had a winner!

I coughed the dirt out of my lungs as I picked up the telephone.

"Hello" — gasp — "Mrs. Hale?"

"Yes. Who is this?"

"It's Bekah." — cough — "I have a problem …"

After I assured her that I didn't have the bubonic plague and I wasn't contagious, she said I could borrow the vacuum.[3]

"I'll be right there," I said.

It only took a few moments to drive the short distance to her house. I picked up the vacuum and headed home. Soon I was cooking with Crisco; no problems. But somehow I'd forgotten that tragedies come in groups of three.

"I'll be right back," I told Mom when I finished cleaning. "I'm just taking the vacuum back."

"Okay." She smiled.

Everything was fine until I delivered the vacuum and got behind

---

2. All good barfing begins with burping. Little hiccups, you know.
3. If I wore a mask.

the wheel of the car. It was then that I saw the ant. He was on my foot, making his way up my leg.

"Stupid ant," I muttered.

I'm not sure exactly what happened next. I only know there was a loud noise and a sick feeling in the pit of my stomach. A very sick feeling. Suddenly, I knew how the vacuum felt when it vomited in the backseat of my car. Only now, I was in the front seat and my head was spinning like a washing machine on the fastest cycle.

In a split second, I'd collided with a tree. There was smoke coming from the hood; there was fluid pouring from the engine; there was a crack the distinct shape of my head in the windshield.

"No," I groaned, "this cannot be possible … No! No! No!"

My first accident, and it just had to be in my neighbor's yard. The entire world was going to know about this. I had to get away. Fast.

The car wouldn't start, so I ran. Huffing and puffing, I finally made it to our back door. It was then that it hit me — I'd left my keys in the car. This nightmare was only getting worse. I had to ring the doorbell.

"Mom," I sobbed, "don't kill me …"

"What's wrong, baby?"

"In … the … Hale's … tree … there's … a … car …"

"Whose car?"

"My car …"

"Oh, baby." [4]

Mom was able to get the car started. But Mrs. Hale was frantic.

"*Please* don't tell anyone," I pleaded with her. "I'm so embarrassed."

Mrs. Hale held true to her word and told no one. It was our little secret. Meanwhile, long after my dad pulled the last piece of glass from the tree, I was still wondering how all of this had happened.

---

4. Don't mock our southern way of talking.

Accidents Happen ... Even When You're Not Stupid Like Me

The analogy's pretty clear here: accidents happen.[5] Also, did I mention that when I crashed the car into my neighbor's tree, I didn't even have a driver's license? I wasn't about to report the accident, because, sadly, I knew my insurance wasn't going to pay for it. I only had a permit. I didn't want to go to jail.

In the same way, people say sex is great as long as you have a permit (read: "birth control"). But we all know that's not necessarily true. Take a peek at these words from the government:[6]

"The most reliable way to avoid infection is to not have sex."[a]

And:

"Hormonal methods of birth control (such as the pill) and barrier methods (such as condoms) can reduce the risk of pregnancy, and condom use with every sexual act can greatly reduce — though not eliminate — the risk of STDs."[b]

I realize the above information probably isn't a huge news flash, because we all know that sex with multiple partners has risks. But in the words of my good friend, Crystal (who found out she was pregnant during her freshman year of college), "I knew about the risks. I guess I just didn't think it would happen to me."

I think that's our problem, isn't it? We don't think it can happen to us. But Crystal, who is now raising a son by herself, learned that safe sex wasn't a guy who paused to put on a strawberry-flavored

---

5. Especially in relationships.
6. Boring, I know, but don't tune me out just because I used the word *government*.

condom. It's a guy who says, "*You* are worth waiting for. I am here *with you*, through whatever comes."

Seriously.

SPOTLIGHT
Fiction by Melissa Nesdahl and Pam Stenzel

I couldn't believe I was actually doing this. I was the good girl. The straight-A student. The confident one who stood in front of the student body as class president.

"Excuse m-m-me, nurse."

The words wouldn't form. My tongue felt like jelly.

Just spit it out.

"Could I please get a condom?"

As the words fell from my mouth, my face grew redder than the cherries I had for lunch.

Please, Lord, just get me outta here.

Tucking the square wrapper into my hand and covering it with her own, the nurse commended me. "I'm glad you're being safe. And, don't worry, this is confidential."

Too bad it couldn't be confidential from God. Two years earlier, I committed to purity at my church retreat. When I stood at the altar, white would mean something. My body would be for my spouse alone. Chemistry at its finest.

Then I met Chris. His smile made my knees go wobbly, and his words promised me we'd be together forever. He asked what kind of diamond I wanted, and I heard "forever."

Soon I would be at the altar. With Chris.

Sex was justified, right?

Prior to graduation, I went to the doctor for my college physical.

Awkward. Since Chris was my only partner, I said nothing about my sexual activity. Besides, the nurse was proud of me. I was safe.

A couple days later, the phone rang.

"Chelsea, you have human papilloma virus, also known as HPV, and need to come in for further testing. This is a sexually transmitted disease."

My mind spun. *Me?* I was "safe." I used a condom. How in the world did this happen?

Now putting on that awkward gown is the least of my concerns. I've already had my cervix frozen twice to prevent any possible cancer cells from growing, and my ability to have children one day is in question. Whenever a guy seems attracted to me (Chris, of course, moved on to his next gorgeous, gullible catch), I immediately push him away. What am I supposed to say: "If we marry one day, you'll most definitely get genital warts and might not be a daddy?" *That* is awkward.

I wish I'd read your book before meeting the good lookin' guy with all the right words. No "safe sex" invention is ever going to keep you perfectly safe, or evade God's safe plan.

✳ ✳ ✳

Flee Youthful Lusts … or the Government. Take Your Pick.

It pains me to admit this, but I love magazines. I was sucked into one that fateful day — the day I sorted through the junk mail and missed a sort-of-important piece of paper.[7]

I was so enthralled with the whole makeup article, the "Are You a Good Kisser?" quiz, and the "Summer's Sexiest Looks" piece that I set aside the junk mail where I always put the junk mail — in the drawer to be sorted later.[8]

---

7. If you call "life-saving" important.
8. Aka 2025.

Turns out I had no idea that my decision to read up on kissing could send my new husband to jail.

Now you know I'm dramatic, but I'm just telling the facts this time. It was a few months after that fateful girl-magazine-reading day when my man decided to do our taxes. Boring, I know, but it turned out the county government wanted more from us than money.

Turns out they wanted my husband. In jail.

You see, on that little piece of paper that I overlooked from the sheriff said, "Failing to report could result in fines or prison sentencing."[9] Turns out the government takes not showing up for jury duty pretty seriously. And my new husband had missed his duty — by about three months.

It pays to know a lawyer. We called him just to be sure we were in the safe zone.

"It's the weekend," Lawyer Guy said, "and it's been three months, and it's very likely that if a deputy gets bored, he's going to show up on your doorstep tonight."

The words *very likely* sent chills down my spine. I am ashamed to admit what happened next.[10] Since it was Friday night and the courthouse was closed and we couldn't exactly explain what happened to a judge yet, we ran. I packed our bags and drove my husband like a fugitive from the law.[11]

We fled.

Which is exactly what I'm telling you to do. Not from the government. That's probably not the smartest move. I'm telling you to flee from lust (1 Timothy 6:11). Run. Get away. Don't put yourself in a position to decide whether you need to use a condom. Don't get

---

9. I'm pretty sure "prison sentencing" didn't mean him writing a book about prison. Hardee-har-har.
10. But for the sake of good storytelling, I will.
11. But if anyone asks, we were simply going for an impromptu visit to the in-laws — right?

alone with a guy you find attractive. (For some reason, girls always laugh when I say that at conferences — but hey, it's really the best form of birth control.)

Run Fast.

You can't do this running thing alone. Like my man and I, you're going to need the help of a vehicle. God is that vehicle. When you give your heart, mind, body, and soul to Jesus, your attempts to run toward his best for you will succeed. His plans for you are for good and not for evil — to give you hope and a future (Jeremiah 29:11). In fleeing lust, you are choosing to walk away when you feel tempted. You are putting one foot in front of the other and leaving the situation. You are not staying behind just to see what happens, or how much you can get away with. In the process, you are not only leaving behind what might harm you, you're running *toward* something better.

I know it's hard to do. But it's worth it. Because for me, running away from temptation meant I was running toward my dream guy, even before we met.

Safe Sex Begins with a Safe Heart

The moment I saw him, I knew he was "the one." Hey — I didn't even believe in "the one." I don't know how to explain it. Something snapped.[12]

I'd heard people use the words "the one," but I just rolled my eyes. There was no "one," I thought. There was only "someone," or several "someones," not one "just-right" guy.

I went straight to stalking him.[13]

---

12. No, not in my brain.
13. There is, after all, only one letter's difference between *talking* and *stalking*.

My family could not have been more shocked. I called my mom from work. "I'm in like," I said. "Serious like. With my future husband."

Mom was calm. Dad was another story. "Just remember," he said, "keep your heart."

I'd been told to keep my heart before. It seemed like a bizarre statement to me. How could I do that yet allow myself to fall in love?

Turned out I had to learn that lesson through a cardboard box.

Don't Live in the Box

I'm not the type of girl who likes to be put in a box. But on a warm day in the mountains of North Carolina, my friend Laura talked me into it.

Literally.

"It'll be fun," she said. "Just crawl in."

I questioned my sanity immediately. I questioned it as I watched the cardboard flaps close. I questioned it as my lungs inhaled the dust mites.[14] I questioned it as my throat gasped for air. I questioned it as my mind screamed, *Get me out of here!*

But it was too late. Laura was in the front seat of the car, and I was in the back. The box and my body slammed into the sideboard every time we rounded another mountain curve.

This will be worth it, I told myself silently, so as not to breathe too much precious oxygen. *This will be worth it.* Then I prayed another silent round of "If I should die before I wake."

Finally, we arrived at our destination. The car engine died, and Laura shouted, "I'll be right back!"

The door slammed again, and I soon realized that my friend was on the Lord's time. After all, the Bible said a thousand years felt like a day to God. Apparently it felt that way to Laura too, since she seemed to be taking her sweet time.

---

14. Gross.

"Where are you?" I groaned. "Get me out of here!"

The next fifteen minutes were the longest of my life.

You don't have to do this, sanity whispered. *You can bust out of this joint.*

I wiped the sweat away from my forehead. "No," I whispered back. "This will be worth it. This will be worth it."

Finally, I heard voices. Real ones. Not like the crazy dialogue going on in my head. I heard the car door open and my friend Marianna ask, "What's in there?"

"Open it," Laura said.

Suddenly the cardboard parted, and I could breathe again. I stuck my hand out and grabbed Marianna's arm.

"Ahhh! It's a *person*!" she screamed. "Ahhh! It's Bekah!" I crawled out of the box, and Marianna nearly collapsed onto the pavement.

We had succeeded. The surprised look on our friend's face was totally worth it. It was worth the wait.

I bet you think you know what I'm going to say here. You think I'm going to tell you that waiting for sex is like being cooped up in a box, but it's so worth the wait.

Wrong.

It's not at all like being cooped up in a box. "Safe sex" — aka abstinence — is not constraining. It's not a lack of sun and fresh air. It's not at all like a cardboard box. Guarding your heart by running from temptation isn't abuse.

It's *freeing*.

So what does the box represent? This might surprise you, but the box represents sex outside of marriage.

"Whatever," you might be thinking. "Isn't discovering yourself sexually a carefree thing to do?"

Yes. If that sexual discovery happens in a relationship where you are free to be you. Where you are loved unconditionally. Where you can give yourself fully and completely.

So even when people might tell you what you're missing out on by not using their version of "safe sex," or that you're closed off, suffocating, stuck in a box — you can know there's so much more to a deep relationship than sex. Don't get me wrong — I love sex. But as Americans we have it all backward. We start with sex and then figure out we're bad at talking. There's chemistry but nothing more.[15]

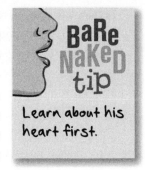

Learn about his heart first.

What if we learned each other's hearts *before* we touched each other's bodies? Jesus said the truth is what sets us free. Satan wants us to believe the lie that sex outside of marriage frees us. But the truth is, sex outside of marriage is what creates chemical bonds to multiple people (remember the study in chapter one?).

So I'm challenging you today: let's step outside the box. Let's leave behind the constraining things other people are saying to us about sex. Let's choose to be free — free to breathe, laugh, stretch — and of course, dance.

Free to Dance

I wasn't prepared when Josh asked me out. Not on a date. We were just friends. But one day as we were hanging out as friends,[16] he said, "Hey, wanna experience some culture?" And because it was the middle of my senior year and I was feeling particularly bored,[17] I said, "Um. Okay."

I was beginning to question my decision as I walked with him toward the house. First, there was the smell. Either this place was

---

15. And then we wonder why people are falling "out of love" so easily.
16. Have I said that enough?
17. No offense, Josh — you're lots of fun to hang out with.

actually a zoo or people were eating organic. And since I was in Asheville, North Carolina,[18] my second guess was correct. I've never seen so much garlic in one place.

Second, there was the noise. I use the word *noise*, because, for the first time in my life, I lacked words to actually describe something. But if I had to try, I would say the sound was somewhere between a herd of elephants and a rock band, with ear-splitting demon-possessed screams in between.

I walked through the empty kitchen to the deck.

This is when I realized I'd better leave now if I valued my ears or my feet. And a preppy girl does value her feet, especially when she's been told her polish is so perfect she could be a toe model.[19]

There was only one problem. As I watched the people dance — no, stomp — I realized I liked Josh. No. Not that way. As a friend, I told you. And since I valued his friendship, and these people were also his friends, I could at least be kind. (The truth is, I was terrified.)

I found my way to the edge of the porch, asking myself important questions, such as but not limited to, *Where is the safest place to be if this porch goes down from overcapacity?*

I refused to think about it. I also refused a lot of offers to dance. I liked to think that the guys kept asking because I was cute. But the truth is, I shaved. And there aren't many hippies who are attracted to people with smooth legs (I learned this fact later). They, too, were being kind.

Then it happened.

The kindness subsided. There was no alcohol involved in this moment, I swear. I was sitting peacefully on my ledge like a bird when a stranger grabbed my arm. Then his dance partner grabbed my other arm and two other people grabbed my feet. (Really — I

---

18. Aka Hippie Central.
19. Not that I'm bragging. Okay, I am.

weighed about eighty-nine pounds at the time. How many hippies did they think it would take to lift a twelfth grader?)

Soon I was in the midst of eighty-nine twirling, swirling, sweaty bodies. I felt the panic coming on. *"But I can't dance!"* I shouted. "I don't know what to do!"

"Just move your feet!" the bearded stranger[20] shouted back. "That's all you have to do!"

The control freak in me died at the moment. It was either kill the freak or kill my body by making a false move. The music played, and my toes started to move, at first in an effort to get away from the powerful smells of other bare feet. (You never know what kind of fungus you might catch from someone else's toenails.) Then something surprising happened.

I actually started to feel a rhythm. I probably looked like a fool to everyone else, but my feet were actually keeping time. I didn't freak out when a hairy armpit brushed up against my shoulder.[21] I didn't notice as time passed that eventually I'd been dancing ... and dancing ... and dancing until the music stopped and my feet were stinging with splinters.

At some point during the dance festival,[22] the sky opened up. No, I mean it. It really opened up. And for the first time in a long time, I saw the stars. I felt the cool night air. I knew my body was alive.

I was free.

Me — Miss Prep — found herself in the middle of the woods dancing barefoot on a sagging back porch. And loved it.

Sometimes it's surprising the things that set us free. We were made to dance. We were made to give our hearts fully. We were made to feel alive.

Sex outside of marriage may make us feel just a flicker of what we

---

20. Who I think was about twelve years old.
21. Okay, I freaked out. A little. But I didn't scream.
22. I made those words up, as I never did learn what barefoot hippies call these things.

think it is to be alive. But in the end, condoms, pregnancy worries, STD freak-outs — they tie us to the back porch. They keep our feet from finding the real dance. The one that will allow us to enjoy sex the way God wanted it: Unchained. Unboxed. Free.

The way it was designed to be.

(UN)SCIENTIFIC QUIZ

How Desperate Are You?

1. Your friends tell you you're an idiot to wait for marriage. You:
    a. Ignore them and change the subject.
    b. Show them a documentary on the benefits of waiting.
    c. Give your reasons and move on.

2. You see a really romantic movie and you:
    a. Turn off the movie and go to sleep like nothing happened.
    b. Write in your diary to your future husband.
    c. Have vivid dreams about making out all night.

3. You have a crush on your best friend. You:
    a. Go on like everything's normal.
    b. Walk around humming Taylor Swift's "Teardrops on My Guitar."
    c. Give subtle hints, like leaving notes in his locker.

4. It's prom night. You:
    a. Do the dress and the limo thing. After all, everyone else is doing it.
    b. Are so prepared. You picked out your dress two years ago. And your date. He doesn't have an option — you asked him when he was twelve.
    c. Asked your best friend a couple of weeks ago.

BARE NAKED RESULTS

Mostly a's: You're well balanced. But you might be putting on a little bit. Make sure you're not denying your emotions and living in an emotionally constipated stupor.

Mostly b's: You're a little dramatic. You could just be a deep feeler, or you could be a little too focused on the whole relationship thing. Take a step back and try to focus on the other amazing parts of your life.

Mostly c's: Congrats. Your subconscious is telling you that you're interested in relationships, but you're not so focused on having relationships that you can't enjoy other parts of your life. You're well on your way to finding your balance.

BARE NAKED JOURNAL

When you think of freedom, what snapshot comes to mind?

_____

_____

_____

What would you like your future relationships to look like?

_____

_____

_____

What's your battle plan for when someone wants you to give into the lie of "safe sex"?

_____

_____

_____

LIE #5

I'm the Perfect Virgin

NEVER THOUGHT I'D END up in jail. Somehow it just wasn't on my A list. So you can imagine my shock when one moment I had no criminal record and the next moment I was a … felon.

That's right.

It started out as a normal day. School. Homework. Retail therapy. My feet hit the mall floor one at a time, pounding out the frustrations of the day. It was then that I heard it.

"Hold on to this for a minute."

Okay. Once again my sister was treating me like a pack mule. Um, I'm pretty sure this shopping trip was supposed to be about me. So why was I following her around like a slave? Any younger sisters out there? Can I see a show of hands? You know what I wanted to say at that moment: "Carry it yourself."

I just didn't say it out loud.

Let me explain. I am about three feet tall. My sister is exactly one foot taller than me, but her arms are so long they wrap around my body.[1] I wasn't about to say what I was really thinking. So, instead, I thought it. And walked away.

I was browsing through the pens like the writer-nerd I am[2] when once again my sister injected herself on my retail therapy. "Let's go."

I obeyed silently, but my brain screamed, *Sure. Go ahead. Tell me what to do. Everyone else does. Mom, Dad, you, our brother, my teacher …* I was so busy reciting my mental list of possible tyrants that I didn't even notice I'd walked right out the front door of the store. With my sister's property in my hands. Only it wasn't her property. Because she hadn't paid for it.

Neither had I.

Have you ever tried to explain to a police officer that it was just a lapse of thinking that made you shoplift? Have you ever seen the look on an officer's face when he says, "That's what they all say"?

Thankfully, I didn't have to see that look. Apparently, the printer paper I was holding (Yes, I shoplifted printer paper — how lame is that? How come I didn't go for a Rolex?) didn't actually have a security tag on it. I texted all the way home in my sister's big red Buick (also known as "Les" for LeSabre) before my sister said, "Rebekah Joy."[3]

"What?" I asked innocently — and meaning it.

"What have you done now?"

I looked at my lap and panicked. The kind that takes your breath away and leaves you looking for the closest stash of oxygen.[4] I stared over my shoulder, waiting for blue flashing lights, or lightning to strike me down.

---

1. Four times.
2. Who browses pens at the mall? Really?
3. That's how I knew I was in trouble. My sister always tried to sound like my mom.
4. Or ribs and fries.

I was the pastor's kid. I could just see the front page of the small city newspaper. Me, staring through the bars of the local jail cell, handcuffed to a Bible the congregation brought me right before my execution.[5]

Okay, so I was being a little dramatic. In the end, I carried the paper back into the store and handed it to a cashier with trembling hands.[6] She looked at me like I was the stupidest person she'd ever laid eyes on.

"I took this accidentally," I said. And then I walked away.

If only all mistakes were so easy to undo.

I tell you this story[7] because it reminds me of how easy it is to turn off your brain and go through the motions of life like I did. The only problem is, when you turn off your brain, eventually you're going to do something stupid. And no, I'm not just talking about shoplifting.

I'm talking about going too far with a guy.

Maybe you've "saved" yourself for marriage and you've always thought you would continue to do so. Maybe you *know beyond a doubt* that this is your intention. You have your lines. You even have step-by-step plans all laid out.

Can I tell ya something? Get out of autopilot!

Just because you've made this decision doesn't guarantee 100 percent that you will succeed. You are going to meet someone. You are going to like someone. You are, like me, going to want to do sexual things with someone. Trust me.

Get out of autopilot.

I'm not gonna lie. The first thing I noticed about my now-husband is that

---

5. Execution by church, not local government.
6. Mine, not hers.
7. Yet another one that makes me look like an idiot.

he's attractive — tall, Swedish, blue-eyed, muscle-bound attractive. My first thought was that I wanted to take his hand, walk him into the woods, and kiss him like he'd never been kissed before — among other things. (This is a little embarrassing to say, because I know his mother will be reading this. But I'm just being honest here.[8])

It wasn't easy to wait for marriage. Especially after we got engaged. We knew we wanted to have sex, and we knew it was eventually going to happen. So why not get just as close as we could? But we also knew we wanted to wait, and it was difficult enough to stick with kissing.

We knew from experience that things can go really far really fast. Which is what Allison wants to talk to you about next. Allison? You're up.

SPOTLIGHT
Allison

When I came to college my freshman year, I fell in love with a boy on the football team whom I met through some dorm activities. He was cute, sweet, and caring. Over time I gave my heart to him. People said that on weekends and after games, he would go out with his friends and party and drink and sleep around, but when he was with me, he wasn't like that.

Around me he was Prince Charming. A perfect gentleman, he was very slow with adding any form of physical touch to our relationship. We didn't even kiss until after about six months of being together. One night, one year into our relationship, he invited me to his apartment. We were talking about the future and plans and dreams, and then it just happened. We started kissing, and one thing turned into another.

---

8. You make gorgeous kids, Sue. Oh, and you too, Bill. I mean … um … Dr. Martin. Um … Mr. Dr. Martin.

In my head I was thinking, *This isn't right. You shouldn't be doing this. When are you going to stop?* All the things I had learned from growing up in a strong Christian family popped into my head, and I was just *so torn* inside. I knew this was not a path I wanted to go down, but at the same time, I wanted to make this guy I loved happy! I wanted to please him the way he always pleased and cared for and made me happy.

Well, at a certain point, my boyfriend asked me, "How far are you willing to go tonight?" and I went extremely close to having sex. Let's just say my clothes were off, his clothes were off, etc. I think you get the picture. But I finally stopped just before we actually had intercourse.

Time went on, and my boyfriend turned more and more to alcohol to solve his problems rather than to me. I finally gave him an ultimatum — either me or drinking. Well, you know what he chose. After we broke up, I was heartbroken. I was hurt. I felt used, betrayed, embarrassed, etc. Even now I have so much trouble trusting men in general. I gave this boy a special part of me, and he just threw it to the wind.

It hurts. Every day, it hurts. However, what I have come to realize after much prayer, counseling, etc., is that if you really care about each other, the commitment of waiting until marriage is worth it in the end.

I wish I had waited. I thought it would be cool to lose my virginity because everyone around me had. Now I realize the girls who are holding on are not prudes or weird but are special and strong. It takes courage and guts to save yourself — and guys admire that about a girl.

* * *

But I'm Smarter Than That ... (Are You Judging?)

"Please," she said, "just get rid of it."

It sounded like a good plan to me. So I tossed "it" into the woods. After all, quitting smoking would probably save her life some day.

Only what I didn't think about was …

Her withdrawals would start today. On a remote mountainside. At a Christian summer camp.[9] So I did what any other good friend would do: I told my buddy she was going to have to tough it out.

Have you ever dug through the underbrush at one in the morning without a flashlight, grasping at anything that smells remotely like tobacco?

Me neither. I just (temporarily) wanted to make it sound like I at least tried to be sympathetic. The truth is I didn't really understand what my friend was going through. Did I feel bad? Yeah. But my feeling had limits, quite frankly, because I had never "been there." My intentions were okay, but I couldn't imagine shaking through the withdrawals in the other cabin — all night long.

I've seen a similar attitude lately at camps/youth groups/Christian places. Not about tobacco, but about other addictive behaviors. The attitude that says, *Why don't you just find the willpower to stop doing this to your body?* Some Christians are telling girls to stop having sex without giving them the tools to quit. What bothers me most, though, is when that attitude evolves into an attitude of judgment. *I'm better than you. How come you can't be more like me?*

You know what I'm talking about. There's often a definite clique of "good girls" who separate themselves from the "bad girls." Girls with a past are often treated as sluts. So many times I see the good girls throw the metaphorical tobacco into the woods as a fast fix — rather than reaching out and trying to help restore the broken through gentleness.

The Bible is very clear about this: "Brothers and sisters, if someone is caught in a sin, you who live by the Spirit should restore that person gently. But watch yourselves, or you also may be tempted" (Galatians 6:1).

---

9. Asking for a nicotine patch would be like asking for a quick tour of the moon.

In other words, *it can happen to us*. It only takes seconds for things to get out of control. We might think it can't happen to us, that we'll never put ourselves in that situation. But judging others opens the door for us to fall as well.

God's heart is all about restoration. He wants to see us open our arms to help him heal the repentant and the broken. In fact, his heart for the lost is so big that Jesus said this about his life's mission: "The Spirit of the Lord is on me, because he has anointed me to proclaim good news to the poor. He has sent me to proclaim freedom for the prisoners and recovery of sight for the blind, to set the oppressed free" (Luke 4:18).

He also said, "It is not the healthy who need a doctor, but the sick. But go and learn what this means: ' … I have not come to call the righteous, but sinners'" (Matthew 9:12 – 13).

Jesus craves a relationship with those who have wandered from him. He says he is like a shepherd who leaves ninety-nine obedient sheep in the field to go after one sheep who has wandered from him. And most of us know at least one wandering sheep who has been turned out of the fold by her "Christian" family and friends.

What are we doing for those sheep? How can we help them find Jesus through gentleness? I've turned to Madison to help me understand what girls who have wandered out of the fold might be feeling — and why some of them may have wandered in the first place.

SPOTLIGHT
Madison

On the outside, I looked like I had it all together — I was a mentor and worship leader in my youth group, after all. I wanted to follow Jesus with everything I had, but things at home weren't what they seemed.

My parents were very strict. They demanded "purity" from me and my sisters in every sense of the word. We weren't to talk with boys, think about boys, or even spend time in "mixed groups." They even told us, "The only thing men want from you — whether it is the seven-year-old boy you babysit or the eighty-year-old retired pastor who lives next door — is sex. It doesn't matter what they say, how they act, or what you think. That is really all they want."

I didn't think that sex was all the boy at church wanted. He sent me a letter — just a simple note of friendship — and my parents intercepted it. They woke me up that morning, screaming at and berating me. They called me names and told me I would get pregnant.[10] Eventually, I stopped telling them things altogether. Evidently, my purity was nearly lost irrevocably in their minds — simply for talking with the opposite sex.

I found out years later that my dad had found and threatened my crush. He told the boy that he would make his life miserable if he ever so much as dreamed of contacting his daughter again. Little did my dad in his "wisdom" know that this "rebellious" boy would grow to be a brilliant, mighty man of God who had a heart for healing broken people.

Broken people like I was about to become.

There were other boys. I grew better at hiding my feelings from my parents, though it didn't seem to matter. They somehow always found a way to discover what was going on with me — whether it was

---

10. From talking to a boy?

reading my journal, intercepting my mail, or searching my room. More screaming and verbal abuse ensued.

Looking back, I realize that I was a really good kid. I obeyed the letter of the law, but it was never enough. The standard that had been set was so impossibly high, and the verbal attacks I suffered on an almost daily basis drove me into a deep depression. I felt worthless. Like there was no hope. I believed I was capable of no good. I was no good. If my worth was wrapped up in my mental purity, then I had destroyed that, because I had given my heart to more than one boy. The only thing I had left to hold on to was my physical purity.

Soon even that was gone.

I met a guy who was older than me. He said he was in the process of starting a rescue mission in India. He was handsome and confident and said all the right things. I was smitten and became convinced that if I married him, we could make a difference together. Over time I grew to trust him completely.

Eventually, we became more and more physical. We flirted with the line of what was fooling around and what was going all the way. I trusted him completely. Until the day my last bit of self-worth was whisked away in the span of about ten seconds. There, in a garage, over a pile of dirty laundry like the cheap whore I was made to feel like, it was gone. He knew I had wanted to wait for that. He knew I was a virgin. But it didn't matter. My "purity" was gone along with any shred of self-worth I had left. I believed I was now officially nothing.

I went home feeling completely empty. There was no way my parents could know. They had screamed at me over a letter from a boy — this was far worse. I had to just move on and keep trying to pretend that I hadn't just been destroyed, but it didn't work. I confessed with tears to my youth pastor's wife what had happened. She prayed with me. Then word got out to my circle of church friends that I was "promiscuous." My fate was sealed. I was now the resident whore.

The pastor's wife asked me to take a break from youth group. I understood and repented, and to be honest, the break felt like a relief. When I finished the allotted time we'd talked about, however, I was not welcomed back. I was told I was not allowed to speak to or pray with any of the girls who had been my friends.

> "The same youth pastor's wife who had just banned me from youth group ... prayed that we would have compassion on the hurting."

One night I went to prayer meeting, and the same youth pastor's wife who had just banned me from youth group stood up in front of the room and prayed that we would have compassion on the hurting. That we would be the hands of Jesus in broken people's lives and would be used to heal wounded hearts. I lost it. I stood up and walked out of the prayer room. On my way home, I called her cell phone and left a seething message "apologizing" for not having been better at sucking up to her and fitting into her "perfect little clone club" among other things. It was very wrong of me. I should not have done it, but it was how I felt. The person who was supposed to be helping me move forward was talking about me behind my back.

The depression I had been managing for years raged with a new-found fury. The screaming bouts with my mom were getting worse. *All* of my friends abandoned me except one — a guy who had been a confidant to me. He was there for me. He comforted me. He held me.

Then our friendship turned physical.

This new relationship would mark the beginning of a new pattern in my life that brought me to my most desperate moment. The only friend I had left wanted me for booty calls. He was at least honest about it, but he really did only want me for one thing. I decided that must be all I was worth anymore — a good lay. So that's what I became.

There were a few months in there when I would get sloppy drunk and have indiscriminate sex with random guys. I'm not proud of this fact. I'm actually growing nauseous as I write it because it sickens me to think of who I was then. I hated that girl. I was a lost, sick pup who would turn to anyone who might make her feel a little attractive and worthy of attention at least for a little while. For a time, I

> **"If all I had been good for was to be a perfect virginal bride, and that was gone, then what *was* I good for?... I might as well have a little fun, right?"**

actually felt empowered by the fact that I could get any guy into the sack.[11] I got to the point where I would use men specifically to hurt them. I had lost the ability to love. If all I had been good for was to be a perfect virginal bride, and that was gone, then what *was* I good for? Exactly nothing. So I might as well have a little fun, right?

And then one night I reached bottom. I found myself riding in the back of a car with my other wild-child friend and three guys we had met that night in a bar. Our designated driver had almost run off the road multiple times, was going at least ninety-five, came within inches of multiple cars, and was swerving worse than I can begin to describe. It turned out that he had been popping Ecstasy all night and was further gone than any of the rest of us. I knew I was going to die, and my parents would have no clue where I was or who I was with. Nevertheless, we, by the hand of God, arrived unscathed at our destination, although our destination couldn't have been further from anywhere God wanted me.

It was that night in a foreign bed in a strange room, lying next to a guy whose last name I didn't even know, that I lay staring at the ceiling crying bitter tears of hurt, disillusionment, and fear. I felt trapped

---

11. If guys could be players, why couldn't girls?

> "It turned out that he had been popping ecstasy all night and was further gone than any of the rest of us."

and couldn't wait for the morning to come. I was imprisoned that night in the room — not by that guy, but by my broken life, and by bad decision upon bad decision. I got out of bed and stared at myself in the bathroom mirror. Who had I become? I was a whore. And I hated myself with a fiery passion. There were several times after that night, while taking a bath, that I would hold my breath and go underwater to see how it would feel to just end it all.

Something had changed inside me. I knew I had to do something drastic and fast or I would do something truly stupid. I swore off men, enrolled in a college in another state, and got a job — standing on my own two feet for the first time. Getting out and away was one of the best things I could have done. While I was there, I met a guy who was unlike any guy I had ever met before. He was a genuine friend to me in a way I never knew possible. He was kind to me; he listened to me. He respected me. He loved me and went out of his way to show me. He asked my opinion about things, and he let me speak my thoughts. He let me pour out my heart to him and was with me not because of what he could get from me, but for what we could be together. It took a long time for me to pull down my walls and allow him to love me — or to allow myself to give my heart to him. Because of my past, my lack of self-worth, and the hurt I had suffered at the hands of selfish men, I really struggled with the idea that someone could love *me*. Hadn't I given all that was valuable away already? Why would he want someone who was anything but "pure"?

I began to understand that he *did* love me. When I tried to push him away, he loved me. When I tried to run, he loved me. When I struggled with trusting, he was patient and he loved me. I finally knew what unconditional love looked like. He picked me up out of the mud;

he cleansed my heart with his love. He forgave me when in my hurt I hurt him. Sound familiar? He showed me redemption.

"He respected me."

After we had dated for a few years, he asked me to be his bride. I joyfully accepted. It took a lot of time and patience, but gradually he showed me that *my virginity did not define my worthiness.* Nor did the feelings I had or refrained from having affect my purity. In fact, my past — though regrettable — had actually played a part in shaping me into the woman I am today. And even beyond all of that, he helped me see that I am a beautiful, lovely woman. I am priceless. I have worth in not only my husband's eyes, but also in God's eyes. As amazing, loving, and merciful as my husband was to me, God was infinitely more so.

It has taken some time, but over the years I have forgiven my parents and my church friends, and I love them dearly. I also know that they love me and really were trying to do the best they could with what they believed. But I am also saddened when I see the same things happening in other churches. I think of that girl — me — who started losing my hair at the time because my stress level was so high. It was after that that I pretty much threw caution to the wind. When I think about the person I became, it would be easy to blame those pastors or even my "friends." But I blame my enemy Satan and my own choices. My friends were misguided. If I could go back to telling them what I needed at the time, it would be this:

1. *Have compassion.* I understand now that the people at my church held me to a higher standard because I was in leadership, but they could have done what they originally offered when they asked me to take a break from the youth group and help me get healing. They could have had me go through counseling or pointed me in the right direction to get help, then welcomed me back.

2. I once heard someone say, "The church is the only community in which we kill our wounded." When a young girl comes forward with an unplanned pregnancy, confession of drug use or abuse, or any manner of cry for help, it breaks my heart. We *must* rush to her side as friends and fellow brothers and sisters. We must show her the love of Christ. After all, who did He have compassion for? The wounded, the infirmed, the sinners, the lepers, the children.

3. *Get them involved in serving in the church.* Meet with them regularly and give them books to read and Scriptures to study, and show them not only how to study but also how to apply those truths to their lives. Taking punitive action in return for honesty is counterproductive. It only teaches girls that they will get punished if they bring their shortcomings to the light. And out of self-preservation, they will not only pull away from you, but quite often also from the church altogether.

4. *Encourage girls to get help from someone they trust.* Don't turn your back on them or think you can't make bad decisions too. The best thing you can do is love your sisters and even go with them to the adult leader (youth pastor, minister, counselor) who can get them the help they need. If you show them that Jesus loves them no matter what, you could be a saving voice inside their head and the only true friend they have.

Finally, it is *vital* that your friends know their worth is not derived from their innocence. That it is not earned from anything they do or refrain from doing. We are valuable because God says we are. He loves us, He created us, and He calls us His children. And that's reason enough to love and reach out to one another.

* * *

We started out the chapter by talking about accidental prisons (remember my shoplifting analogy?). It's true that by judging others like Madison, we can put them in a prison that keeps them from getting the help they need.

But we can also put ourselves in prison by making purity an action rather than a condition of our hearts. There is no such thing as a perfect virgin. We all struggle with our thoughts, if not our actions. So let's release ourselves today from our accidental prisons. Let's focus on the one who can make us pure, rather than on our idea of what purity looks like on the outside. The Bare Naked Journal pages will help us think things through with our hearts.

(UN)SCIENTIFIC QUIZ

Are You a Mean Friend?

1. Your unmarried friend tells you she's pregnant. You:
    a. Smile and nod, while silently naming the first person in your head you're going to tell.
    b. Encourage her to get help.
    c. Offer to help her find someone to talk to.

2. You've never really liked this girl, so you:
    a. Befriend her and then talk about her deep issues to all your friends.
    b. Try to understand where she's coming from.
    c. Sit down and listen from the heart.

3. Your friends are talking about the slutty girl at school. You:
    a. Join in and make some points no one else thought to make.
    b. Listen silently.
    c. Stand up for her; who knows what she's going through?

4. A friend is wearing a slutty top. You:
   a. Make sure all the guys at school know.
   b. Tell her she looks like a whore.
   c. Suggest it's not quite the look she's going for.

BARE NAKED RESULTS

Mostly a's: Congratulations — you're catty. You live in a world that makes you feel better by tearing other people down. But there might be a better way to feel good about yourself: showing empathy to others.

Mostly b's: You walk the middle road when it comes to friendship. You keep silent when sometimes you feel like you should speak your mind. You're not doing a lot of damage to your friends because you're not mean, but it wouldn't hurt to speak up for them every once in a while.

Mostly c's: You're incredibly loyal. You take your friendships seriously and truly care about others from the heart. Just make sure others don't take advantage of your kindness.

BARE NAKED JOURNAL

Name two practical ways you can reach out to a friend who is hurting:

_____

_____

_____

How would you define the "perfect virgin" after reading this chapter?

_____

_____

_____

If you've been shunned by people within a church, how could they treat you differently to help you heal?

_____

_____

_____

LIE #6

It's Okay to Have Sex as Long as You're in Love

I HAVE A CONFESSION: I am scared to death of old people. But before you jump on my case about disrespect,[1] you need to know why my terror exists. I'm embarrassed to admit this, but when I was single, most of my conversations with older men usually ended in dates.[2]

As you can guess, after a couple of really ... um ... interesting blind dates,[3] I began to avoid the whole OPS (Old People Scene). Which is, by the way, really hard to do if you go to church at all,

---

1. Just in case my mother reads this.
2. With their grandsons.
3. Do the words "Italian sushi bar" mean anything to you?

because you can meet anyone at any time. ("Mr. Jones? Yeah ... I hate it that I can't talk right now ... but I'm allergic to the little pencils on this side of the auditorium ...")

Like most people with phobias, I came up with creative ways to avoid these situations. I thought the Illinois Mission[4] was one of those ways. After all, the brochure displayed *young*, bright, smiling volunteers. They were happy. They were under the age of eighty. And most of all, they were male.

I signed up right away.

When I arrived on IM's campus, ready to help out, I realized there was a problem. Apparently "Illinois Mission" was a pseudonym for "retirement center." As far as I could tell, the brochure was a clever marketing ploy to capture teenagers and force them into backbreaking labor, doing things like opening letters.

I arrived at IM late one evening when everyone else was in bed, so my first clue about the place was a nearby bathroom. I stared curiously at the little cups lined along the sink. *Oh, how nice,* I thought. *The mission has given the volunteers cups for their contact lenses.* What I saw next will haunt me until the day I die.[5]

Something was floating in the cups. Something that looked like blue goo and Tic Tacs. Something remotely resembling ... teeth.

The next morning, my fears were absolutely confirmed: The people at breakfast were my age — seventy years ago. Except one girl. She was my age maybe ten years ago. I knew she and I were going to be inseparable. Mostly because I wanted to ask her how to make a jailbreak since I'd already promised IM one week of my life.

I watched the girl traipse across the dining hall, breakfast plate in hand. Was that something rolling around on her dish? I looked closer. A hard-boiled egg? I watched in horror as she placed it in the

---

4. Name and location of this organization changed to protect the guilty. And myself from lawsuits.
5. I'll give you a clue. There wasn't candy in there.

microwave and closed the door. (I'm no scientist, but I did learn, say, back in kindergarten, that hard-boiled eggs + microwaves = bad idea.)

Suddenly I felt like James Bond, ready to stop a train with my bare hands. Only my hands wouldn't move. So I opted for my James-Bond-in-a-coma pose — I closed my eyes and braced for the impact.

Nothing. Happened.

The microwave beeped. My eyes popped open. *Hmm, if my teacher lied to me about the whole hard-boiled egg thing, I might have to sue.*

The girl traipsed back across the room and stuck a fork into the egg. It was like a perfectly timed dance — followed by a gunshot.

There were screams.[6] There were shouts. There were Vietnam vets dashing under tables. There was debris in my eyelashes. On the ceiling. On the floor. And on my shoes.[7] I'd never seen anything like it.

Even so, I wasn't prepared for what happened next.

No one could figure out the cause of the explosion, and the culprit was too shocked to talk. The onlookers knew about the debris. They knew about the egg. But they *didn't* know about the microwave. To be honest, they had no clue what had just happened.

They started to whisper among themselves.

"Don't eat the eggs!" they said. "They're explosive!" I thought their response was hilarious — until I told my friend Amy about it later.

"Well," she said matter-of-factly, "wouldn't you stop eating eggs if you didn't know why they were exploding?"

She had a point. I could eat the eggs confidently because I knew what had happened. I'd seen it with my own eyes. I understood the cause and the effect. But spontaneously combusting eggs aren't the only reason I needed to understand cause and effect at that point in my life. Take for instance, the following chart:

---

6. Mostly mine.
7. I'm pretty sure I saw several people peeling egg out of their nasal cavities.

If I have sex …	Stuff will happen.

See? I made it short so I wouldn't waste your time. Anyone who tells you that being in love makes sex outside of God's design for marriage okay is asking you to microwave a hard-boiled egg. It brings me to this word picture: *Sex outside of marriage is like taking a laxative and a sleeping pill at the same time.*

Sex outside of marriage is always going to result in a mess. I'm not trying to be crass here. I'm trying to say that sex creates a spiritual and emotional bond meant for marriage. Simple cause and effect. But don't take my word for it. Listen to what the apostle James had to say about the topic: "Then, after desire has conceived, it gives birth to sin; and sin, when it is full-grown, gives birth to death" (James 1:15).

Okay, I'm not going to be like an overly dramatic parent here and say, "Sin and you'll die." Sex won't feel like death at first. It'll be like taking a laxative + sleeping pill: you'll have a delayed effect. You won't know how crappy it is until you wake up. In fact, it will probably feel great at first. Liberating. (Remember chapter two and the tanning salon? It seemed like the answer to all my problems — until days later when my skin started to peel piece by piece.)

I'm not going to rehash the consequences of premarital sex in this chapter. (You can skip back to chapter one or ahead to chapter nine if you want to see those.) I'm just letting you know that being in love is not a get-into-bed-free card. Despite the fact that having sex when you're in love will feel good, you're going to be left with the baggage it creates. You can tell yourself until you're blue in the face that you won't have to pay the consequences. Just like I told myself I could fly.

I Believe I Can Fly ... I Believe I Can Touch the Sky ...

It all began when I was about two feet tall. I wanted only one thing in this world: to fly. In my mind, it wasn't fair that pilots flew planes. It wasn't fair that my brother flew model airplanes. And it wasn't fair that birds flew — well, themselves.

I believed that if I wanted to fly badly enough, I could do it. It was just a matter of trying. I'd watched television, and I knew what gravity was. I wasn't about to jump off the roof of my tree house. But it seemed to me that a challenge was a challenge — and I would be the first person ever to defy gravity.

I started small — just in case I needed some practice. The metal bleachers at the softball field were the perfect place. As soon as Dad hit the first home run, all eyes were fixed on the field. Except mine. They were fixed on the pavement below.

Are you sure you want to do this? the sensible part of me asked.

Yes. I had to believe. I could fly.

No one noticed as I hung precariously over the edge of the bleachers ... wondering ... peering ... building faith. No one saw my tiny frame as it leapt into the air...

And stayed there. I could hardly believe it myself. I was flying.

Not very high, mind you. Just a few inches above the ground. I hovered there for a few moments, and then heard it — the dreadful sound. I'd heard it before. It sounded like the time I ripped my dress on the swing.

Only this time I'd caught my underwear.

Now all eyes were fixed on me. You could say I was a little embarrassed. You could say it took the entire softball team to untwist my wedgie. But the truth is I don't remember. I've psychologically blocked the results of my flying attempt. (Apparently, they're just too painful.)

There's a point to the silly story I just shared: *I can believe something with all my heart, but what I believe can still be a lie.*

I believed I could fly. But it couldn't have been further from the truth.

But I'm not five. I know the truth from a lie.

I'm going to give you credit here. I know you're not five years old. I know you know you can't fly. (At least I'm pretty sure you know that.) But there is a lie — a much bigger, much more serious lie the world wants you to believe. It's disguised a lot better, and it's a lot more alluring than most lies.

It's a lie a lot of girls believe — and it's a lie my friend Tricia believed too.

SPOTLIGHT
Author and Speaker Tricia Goyer

If *boy crazy* is a virus, I caught it in the fifth grade and the symptoms lasted for years. I always had a crush on a boy in my classroom, and my daydreams would fill the space between his desk and mine. I daydreamed about my first kiss, about romantic slow dances in the school gym, and even beyond that. I doodled wedding dresses on my math homework and picked out baby names for our children. While other kids planned for a car or a summer job or college, I planned how I would respond when that special someone told me he loved me back.

From fifth to eighth grade, the crushes didn't amount to anything. Not one of the guys I fantasized about liked me. Not one talked sweetly to me over the phone. During this time I read teen romance books and watched all the romantic shows, and as I watched boy-woo-girl, I'd think, "Why can't someone love me like that?"

I was just finishing my eighth-grade year when I found what I'd been looking for. Steven was six feet two inches tall and a sophomore.

Blond hair, blue eyes, handsome smile. He was honestly the cutest boy I'd ever seen. He was the older brother of my friend Tracey, and one day she shared a secret. "I think Steven likes you."

Her hunch was confirmed the next time I visited Tracey's house. While Tracey went to help her mother set the table in the dining room, I got my first kiss on the back porch. Steven's lips were soft, sweet. My heart pounded in my chest. The emotions rushed through me, and it — all of it — was more than I dreamed. I didn't just have a boyfriend; I had Steven. Older, handsome, in-love-with-me Steven.

We dated for months, chatting on the phone and going on walks and kissing. What the movies depicted was true. This was it. Yet before I even started high school, the physical side of our relationship demanded a lot — all of me. I gladly gave myself to him. After all, I was in love. I could feel it. The emotions were real.

The lesson of love, of course, is that as wonderful as falling into it is, having it taken away hurts more than one can imagine. I faced that pain just a few months later when Steven's family moved away. I was heartbroken. I·was empty. I felt as if a part of me had been stripped bare. I didn't realize at the time that it had.

Before then, I didn't consider the reason God had planned sex for the marriage bed — when commitment was sure. When one couldn't be taken away by a parent's move. When a life together could be made into a reality.

The emptiness inside led me to another guy's arms and bed. I ached to feel loved again. Yet the more I gave, the more I lost myself. And when I found myself pregnant at fifteen, my child faced the biggest loss of all — his life when I chose abortion.

I thought finding someone to love me was the answer. I thought our love would last. I thought sex was okay because love made it so. It was only years later when I met my now husband that I realized love wasn't about someone asking me to give everything. When I found true love, it was about someone giving his whole heart and protecting me and honoring me until he committed to be my husband and my lover " 'til death do us part."

* * *

Lie Detector

If Tricia could have detected the lie, she might have avoided some heartache. But like so many of us, she didn't know — how does a girl detect the truth from lies? Is there any such thing as absolute truth?

Let's ask the lie detector.[8]

See, my brother Phil and his friend Mike had a real, honest-to-goodness lie-detector machine when we were kids. We're talking CIA-level legit — it could sense any lie on the planet.

My sister Molly, and Michael's sister Katherine, spent hours hooked up to this lie detector with me. Our brothers would ask us real "truth or dare" questions like "Did you kiss Sammy Farkel under the streetlight at 12:01 a.m.?" And we would answer, "No." Whether or not it was the truth (sometimes there was a false positive, sadly), the lie detector would zap us with an electric jolt more powerful than an exposed power line.

After a few weeks of playing this game, we discovered the lie detector wasn't actually the legit, honest-to-goodness lie detector we'd been led to imagine. Turns out it was actually a doorbell kit, which could not actually detect any lies, since it was sparked manually by our brothers every time they felt like putting two wires together.

---

8. I had to get my brother and his friend Michael to sign about ten releases so I could tell you this story. And then I had to get myself to sign a release stating that, yes, I am the stupidest person in the world.

We were depending on the lie detector to be truthful, but it turned out the source of truth wasn't truthful at all. And that brings me to the moral of this silly story: We need to consider the source of "truth."

Your Truth ... My Truth ... Whose Truth?

I'm going to state the obvious here: If every time we are searching for answers to our questions we turn to Google, *Seventeen* magazine, or our friends, we are going to find something I call relative truth — "truth" that changes. Girls, I have to be blunt here. Relative truth is not truth. It's opinion. And opinion is worth just as much as you pay for it (which, for the magazine you get every month, is about $2.99). Mike and Phil zapped me because they *claimed* I kissed the Farkel kid. It didn't make it true. For something to be true, we have to consider the source of that "truth." And who better to tell us than the creator of the universe — the one who made the rules by which we play?

BaRe NaKeD tip

Saturate yourself in the truth every day.

Girls, you and I are saturated every day with lies from the world. When we hear those lies often enough, we begin to believe they are true. (Again, just because I'm married doesn't mean I'm not tempted by lies. Magazines, television, and even some of my friends tell me things like "It's okay to look at or flirt with another guy. It's just a little innocent fun." It's so easy to let my guard down and give in to it — but not if I want to protect my mind and my marriage.)

If we're going to believe the truth, we have to hear it on a regular basis. That's why it's absolutely imperative that we saturate ourselves

THE WORLD SAYS ...	GOD SAYS ...
Sex is okay if you're in love.	Sex is God's gift inside of marriage. (1 Corinthians 7:2)
Sex is just a physical exchange.	Sex binds you spiritually and emotionally to another person. (2 Corinthians 6:14)
Sex is just a little innocent fun.	You are hurting yourself most of all. (1 Corinthians 6:18)
Premarital sex not really a sin, more like a white lie.	God lists sex outside of marriage with serious consequences, like those of idol worship. (Acts 15:20)
It's your body; you're only hurting yourself.	If you're a believer, everything you do affects God. (1 Corinthians 6:19)
God doesn't really expect you to try abstinence. After all, he wants you to enjoy life.	You should eradicate from your life what God says isn't healthy for you. (Colossians 3:5)

in it. We need to soak it up every single day. When we don't do that, lies begin to sneak in. And like my friend Sarah, we find ourselves paying a costly price:

SPOTLIGHT
Writer and Speaker Sarah Siebert Markley

I got married young on purpose because I wanted to have sex.

As I grew up in church and in youth groups, when we talked about sex, it was held up as this amazing thing that was out there for married people only.

"Married, Married, Married" right next to "Sex, Sex, Sex" kept flashing in my head like one of those neon signs on the Las Vegas strip.

But the problem was that when I met my husband, I was only seventeen. He was eighteen. By nineteen, he'd asked me to get married. I still had a couple more years of college, so we settled in for a long engagement.

I loved him and he loved me, but we both carried some baggage into our relationship. Mine, at the time, was more "carry-on" sized and his was a bit larger, but we were too in love to compare luggage sizes.

Our engagement was well over eighteen months. I did not want to wait a single second longer than necessary, so I planned our wedding for exactly two weeks after I walked to the front of the auditorium in my cap and gown and got my college diploma.

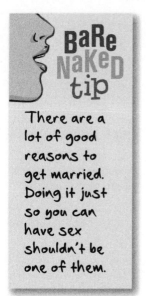

BaRe NaKeD tip

There are a lot of good reasons to get married. Doing it just so you can have sex shouldn't be one of them.

Waiting to have real sex, when we knew we were going to tie the knot, seemed almost impossible. But something inside me barred the way from ever letting it go all the way to intercourse.

It would have been as if I was failing myself, my fiancé, my parents, and every youth group leader who'd told me to wait.

So we did wait.

But we went right up to the edge. Every weekend we engaged in almost anything you can classify as sexual but not actually intercourse. On my wedding night, I was still *technically* a virgin because I'd never actually had intercourse until then.

People will warn us left and right about the dangers of promiscuity before marriage. Mostly, they'll say that by letting ourselves go almost all the way, we rob ourselves of the wonder of it all. They'll remind us we need to keep the marriage bed pure. Maybe they'll add a little guilt on the side.

I think all of that is true, but why my husband and I should have waited is a little different.

There was guilt, sure. And the wonder-thievery when it came to the wedding night? Yes, yes, yes. We'd done everything except putting the "thing" in the "thing" to be very honest, so there wasn't much else to wonder about.

But the worst part about remaining a "technical virgin" was the bad habits that foreplay created in our relationship and the unhealthy patterns I created in my own heart.

By going all the way up to the line and stopping just shy of it, I trained myself to associate that kind of affection and touching with something that was bad and something that was taboo. It took a long time for me to see sex as a holistic thing: something that began with closeness and intimacy and ended in the perfect expression of that intimacy. And four years later, as our marriage began to fall apart, I believe that because of those patterns, I was much more willing to give my body to another man in an adulterous relationship. My heart had become built around "it" and those bad patterns.

Did doing everything but _____ send me straight to hell? Of course not. But it did create a place in me where I was more apt to wander, more prone to have my heart pulled toward other things, and less able to have a healthy marriage in the end.

We're still married and things are pretty good now, but we've had a lot of baggage that we've had to leave at the curb.

* * *

See, lies are tricky things. They can be mixed with half-truths, like Sarah believed, to make them seem more realistic. But the Bible says Satan is roaming around like a lion, seeking someone to devour (1 Peter 5:8). Kind of subtle and creepy — like the invisible squirrels my sister kept seeing.

Lighten Up: People Will Think You're Crazy

My sister was crazy, and there was nothing we could do about it.

"Dad," she said regularly, "they're looking at me!"

By "they," my sister meant the squirrels. They woke her up at night. They hung suspended from her window screens. They stared at her with their black, beady eyes.

Even with three residents upstairs, Molly was the only one tormented by the squirrels. Dad believed her.[9] She was telling the gospel truth, he said. She was stalked by squirrels — even if we couldn't see them.

Dad took extreme measures to keep the squirrels off Molly's windows.

"We're going to cut down that tree," he said one frigid winter day. "If the squirrels can't climb it, they can't get to Molly's windows."

She smiled. Maybe now the squirrels would leave her alone. *Fat chance*, I thought. *It's hard to get rid of something that doesn't really exist.* But it was worth a try.[10]

Drops of sweat dripped down Dad's face as he sawed the stocky tree in two and dragged it into the woods. I searched the limbs carefully for evidence that squirrels had lived there. I wasn't surprised by what I found: nothing. No nests. No acorns. No furry friends.

My family waited anxiously for Molly's appearance at the table the following morning. Red-eyed, Molly took her spot and began to speak. She started with her daily squirrel report, which was as regular as the weatherman's forecast but a lot less accurate.

"They looked at me this morning," she said exasperatedly. "They hung on my window screens again!"

This was almost more than I could bear. *"There are no squirrels!"* I wanted to scream.

---

9. Though I'm pretty sure he believes in the Easter Bunny too.
10. Maybe Molly would stop whining if we played along.

Months passed, and my sister's squirrel stories became fewer and fewer. *Maybe she's forgotten.* I breathed a sigh of relief. *Maybe she's let go of the idea.* But it wasn't long until I discovered the ugly truth.

"What happened to the squirrels?" I asked halfheartedly over breakfast one day.

Molly smiled. "I took the screens off my windows," she said triumphantly, "and the squirrels slid down and fell off the roof." I rolled my eyes but kept my thoughts to myself. Molly was crazy, and there was nothing I could do about it.

Later that day I was horrified to realize the insanity had spread to another member of our family: Dad.

"There are squirrels in my shed!" he said. "They've eaten the insulation!"

They've eaten a lot more than the insulation, I thought. *They've eaten your brain.*

But Dad tacked up nails around the rafters. He sealed doors airtight. He placed poisonous bait in strategic places. But the squirrels were too intelligent.

Or too imaginary, I thought.

A week later, Dad was innocently retrieving tools from the shed. Minding his own business, ignoring the squirrels, and working on a small project.

Did I mention he was standing on a ladder?

Suddenly, a big ball of fur hurtled through the air, straight for his nose. A rabid squirrel.[11]

Dad's heart pounded. His legs weakened. His feet slipped down — down — down toward the floor below. Unfortunately, he collided with the workbench on his way, landing on his back with a painful thud.

Was the furry monstrosity going to attack again? Dad lay there,

---

11. Or so the exorbitant story went.

afraid to move — afraid to breathe. Finally, he crawled quietly toward the door, stood up, and limped toward the house.

The squirrels had won. Or so he said. *I mean, really. Who blames imaginary squirrels for their own clumsiness? I've heard it all now.*

A few days later I realized I could use this whole squirrel thing to get what I wanted. I'd begged for months to repaint my Pepto-Bismol pink room an artsy green. This was my chance.

I headed to the shed for a paint roller.

"Where are you going?" my mother asked.

"To the shed for tools. The squirrels pooped on my walls, and they need repainting."

No one asked any questions. I huffed my way to the shed and opened the door. Suddenly, it hit me — the nauseating smell. My stomached churned. "What in the world?" I whispered.

Then I saw it. There, hanging from the tool rack, was a squirrel — rotting flesh hanging from his carcass. He had missed his target — my dad — and landed fatally on the tool rack. His creepy eyes stared at me.

"*Ahhhhhhhhh!*" I screamed all the way to the house. "You're not going to believe this!" I yelled to Molly. "There are squirrels in the shed!"

My sister looked at me as if I was the dumbest person on the planet. "Where have *you* been?"

I think it's safe to say I was suddenly a believer in the squirrels. It took seeing them with my own eyes, but I knew it was true. And there was no way — no way at all — I would be setting foot in that shed anytime soon. What I believed had changed my actions.

So You Believe in Flying Squirrels?

I've gotta tell you: there is a cost to believing the truth and living it. People are going to look at you like you're crazy. You may be one of the only people in your school to believe that sex outside of marriage is a path you don't want to take. But there is also a cost for not following the truth.

In the Bible, Jesus said, "If anyone, then, knows the good they ought to do and doesn't do it, it is sin for them" (James 4:17). Sin is a price you don't want to pay. It stands between a fulfilling relationship with you and the person who loves you most. It can also stand between a fulfill-

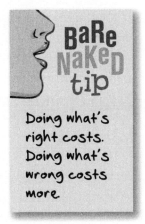

BaRe NaKeD tip

Doing what's right costs. Doing what's wrong costs more.

ing relationship with you and your future spouse. (If you've already walked down this path, you are not alone, and I'm not here to condemn you.) Stephanie knows all about the hope and healing that can happen, even after making decisions she regretted:

SPOTLIGHT
Stephanie Dixon

I was molested by a friend of the family, at the age of eight. Fear silenced me and warped my vision of beauty and love.

At fifteen, even though my parents loved me, I shielded myself with anger to hide my shame. I contemplated suicide, but chose to run away and hide instead.

By my sixteenth birthday, I had plunged into a lifestyle of promiscuity. I correlated sex with love, giving my body away and losing respect for myself. My heart hardened, but the pain didn't dull. The emptiness didn't fade. Being wanted trumped feeling alone and unlovable.

Stuck on self-destruction, I deceived myself into thinking I was in control. That men couldn't take what I willingly gave away. That wall of power and protection crumbled after I was date-raped twice before the age of twenty-one.

I longed to feel safe and loved, but cowered behind feelings of worthlessness and resentment. So, at twenty-three, I married a guy I hardly knew. We slammed headfirst into marriage, both broken and unprepared. My past promiscuity tainted my relationship with my husband, blocking me from experiencing true intimacy.

When I was twenty-five, God blessed us with a son. I cradled him in my arms, afraid to lose him, afraid to hurt him, afraid to let him down. How could I love him if I didn't even know how to love his father, or myself?

It wasn't until my son was in kindergarten that my Savior, Jesus Christ, captivated my scarred heart. God's healing grace began where secret shame smoldered and rage sputtered like molten lava. The Lord empowered me with courage to receive His love, to live the life of freedom and abundance He was offering me. But first, I had to speak.

With my secrets revealed, I didn't believe my husband could really love me. My marriage unraveled. Desperate to give my son a better chance at life, I cried out to God. He answered, "Follow me."

Tired of the emptiness, fear, and dissatisfaction in my life, I drank in God's Word. Truth exposed my wounds to His relentless grace. The Lord helped me forgive the man who had stolen my innocence when I was eight, as well as the men who had raped me. That process seemed easy compared to forgiving myself for the years I abused God's temple, my body.

The Lord peeled off the layers of my guilt, shame, and fear. Nourished and purified by God's unconditional love, a brand-new me evolved. After over thirty-three years of running away and hiding, my vision is clear.

My body is a temple of the Holy Spirit, who is in me, whom I have received from God. I am not my own; I was bought at a price. Jesus paid my debt on the cross. So now I choose to honor God with my body (1 Corinthians 6:19 – 20).

My husband and I are celebrating eighteen years of marriage, devoted to loving God and each other. Our son committed to a vow of purity, breaking the cycle of promiscuity that poisoned my past. Praise the Lord!

I am a valuable child of God, created with purpose. I am forgiven and loved. My life appraised now? Priceless.

* * *

I just love Stephanie's story, because it shows that no matter what's happened in my past — or in your past — God is able to restore our hearts and our emotions. I believe this with everything inside of me, because I have watched Him continue to heal my heart from the molestation that took place in my life.

Maybe you're still on the fence about this whole sex thing. No one's ever taken advantage of you, and you've never given yourself freely either. You're still deciding what you want to do when you do fall in love. So if you're not convinced that waiting's the best thing for you, I'd love for you to meet my *crazy* friend, Aby.

Meet Aby

Aby and I started hanging out our senior year of high school. We clicked immediately. We had the same morbid sense of humor[12] and enjoyed making fun of the same random stuff.[13] I threw a real pity party the next year when she decided to go to college a whole forty-five minutes away from my house.

---

12. She once read me death poetry on my birthday, just to let me know where all these anniversaries were leading.
13. Mainly boys.

"Don't worry," she said. "We can chill at my school when you're free." (What Aby failed to tell me was that having overnight guests in the dorm on school nights was "illegal" at her conservative college — so my visits involved her stuffing me into her closet every time the RA came around.[14])

Once I learned how stale the air in Aby's utility room was, she resorted to calling me instead of kidnapping me. I felt terrible, because while she seemed cool with it, I knew the calling cards were costing her money. Money I didn't have to give, although it didn't stop me from offering.[15] At the end of that year, I got another phone call.

"Hello?"

"You can drop the *o* off the 'hello.'"

"Oh no. Why the mood?"

"You know how I've been buying calling cards to call you all year?"

"Yeah ..."

Here it came. I was prepared. I was going to owe her a total of $342 in long-distance fees.

"Turns out the call isn't long distance."

One day Aby is going to forgive me for telling her story in this book.[16] But I couldn't resist sharing it, because it makes an excellent point: many of us are already paying for something God wants to give us for free. Sex doesn't have to come with a price tag. When we have sex with the spouse God intended for us — within the context of marriage — it comes without the high cost of depression, emptiness, and shame. It comes in its most pure, amazing, mind-blowing form.

---

14. It was like a real-life version of *The Fugitive*.
15. I'm the friend who perpetually "forgets" her wallet at lunch because I'm broke.
16. I have to make fun of other people sometimes, just so it doesn't look like I'm the only one who does this type of stuff.

But to experience the truth, we have to let go of the lie that sex is okay as long as you're in love. Can I challenge you to do that today? Try out these bare naked questions in your journal for help doing that.

(UN)SCIENTIFIC QUIZ

How Well Do You Detect Lies?

1. An Internet chat leads to a conversation about true love. You:
   a. Accept that this chat room guy is the one for you — forever.
   b. Are slightly suspicious of the chat guy's motives.
   c. Tell him he can't get a green card by marrying you.

2. Some kids stop by your house. They say they are collecting money for the poor. You:
   a. Give them all your money.
   b. Ask for documentation before giving a single penny.
   c. Have the part of your doorbell they touched tested for anthrax.

3. Your parents tell you they'll give you $5,000 if you get all A's. You:
   a. Stay up until three in the morning studying.
   b. Study your usual, plus a few hours.
   c. Don't bother — your parents won't have $5,000 set aside by the time they're eighty.

4. A stranger offers you a ride home. You:
   a. Take the stranger up on it and have the time of your life.
   b. Remember that creepy television show and say, "No thanks."
   c. Drop-kick the driver and run for your life.

BARE NAKED RESULTS

Mostly a's: You're gullible (and that's putting it nicely). You easily fall in love and get crushed quickly. You need to stop being so trusting and recognize the ulterior motives others might have.

Mostly b's: A little on the gullible side, but you're doing okay. You don't immediately trust what others say, but you might want to add to your cautiousness just a bit more.

Mostly c's: You're not about living life on the edge. You have some definite caution about whether you're hearing the truth, which is good — but you might want to consider lightening up just a little. Not everyone's out to get you.

BARE NAKED JOURNAL

What are some lies the world wants you to believe about sex?

_____

_____

_____

What are the results of those lies?

_____

_____

_____

What's one cost of saving sex for marriage?

_____

_____

_____

What do you hope will be the benefit of choosing to believe the truth?

_____

_____

_____

LIE #7

Masturbation Will Help Me Save Myself

HEY, LADIES. YUP. You've reached *that* chapter. Don't worry. This isn't health class. It isn't the official talk about … and I'm not going to draw a diagram of your … or his … yeah.

My guess is you probably already have much more sexual knowledge than your parents did at your age.[1] As usual, I'd like to make fun of that fact by telling awkward and immature jokes. But there's a time and a place for all that.

I knew when I wrote this book I didn't just want to entertain you with awkward and immature jokes; I also wanted to share stories with you that would encourage you in the midst of your questions. I wanted to give you resources to pursue in your sexual healing. I

---

1. In fact, you may know more than I do *now* …

wanted you to hear powerful stories of hope from girls who have been where you are and asked the questions you've asked. Questions such as:

- What's the deal with masturbation?
- Is it really addicting?
- Where can I turn for help?

Recently, I received an email that looked a lot like this:

Dear Bekah,
My name is Myra. I'm fourteen. And I'm wondering about masturbation.

I've been "doing it" since I was a little kid. I kind of stumbled on it, and then it became a habit. It's starting to interrupt my life, though. It's all I can think about. When I'm stressed or sad or angry, I have to release that energy.

I can't sleep without it. I didn't used to think it was a problem, but now I'm feeling so alone and scared that this will dominate my life forever.

Does anyone else struggle with this habit? Or am I just a freak?
Myra

I've gotta say, Myra's brave. I'm pretty sure she thought I was going to send her an email back that looked something like this:

Yes, Myra. You are a freak. There is no hope.
Bekah

But the truth is — I had something else entirely to say to Myra. I told her that a lot of girls who come to me struggle with the feeling that sexual thoughts or habits are taking over their lives. That they no longer dominate their urges — their urges dominate them.

Sexual addiction is more common than you might think. Some

girls tell me they got into self-pleasure because it was disguised as stress release. Then masturbation began to create a cycle that looked somewhat like this:

Masturbation Cycle

Wishing to stop

Masturbation trigger

Giving in

Some of these girls were stopping at nothing to get a "fix." Masturbation was a habit that was so engrained in their actual brain chemistry — one they were so dependent on — that they couldn't stop. Even when they wanted to. It became less something they were in control of and more something they had to do in order to remain calm, stable, and balanced.

I'm not saying that everyone who indulges in self-pleasure is going to get addicted to it. But I am saying that if the girls who talk to me are any indication, masturbation's a much bigger issue than some people realize. And for those who have been entrapped by it, it's definitely something that needs to be talked about. One of those girls is my friend Jessica, who not only struggled with sexual addiction for years, but also broke free.

SPOTLIGHT
Jessica

A couple years ago I went to see a stand-up comedian with a friend. Among the various classy[2] segments during her comedy routine, she vividly detailed her fascination as a child with masturbation. The snapshots she illustrated were not limited to the bedroom. I blushed as she

---

2. Note the sarcasm.

talked about masturbating at anywhere from slumber parties to the kitchen table with her family at dinnertime.

I found myself wondering how many girls have had experiences like this. Maybe this stuff happens more than it's talked about. Or maybe I'm the only one who could relate?

You see, I was "that" girl.

Like the comedian, some of my very earliest memories involve masturbation. I don't know how old I first was or why I ever started the habit, but it felt too good to stop. I remember vividly as a very young girl when my mom and her friend walked in on me in my bedroom. After that I grew a lot more careful.

These experiences when I was quite young were only the beginning of what would spiral out of control as I became a teenager. As one might guess, when puberty came, an increased sex drive led to increased acting out. With new intensity, my imagination played an even greater role. Fantasies usually revolved around my crush of the moment. Masturbation began to dominate my time.

Sex and fantasy consumed me. The more I gave in, the more I wanted. Sometimes fantasies would become reality, but my sex-centered relationships never lasted long. It was impossible for anyone to completely live up to my fantasies — including myself. Regardless of how painful the inevitable breakup was, I could always count on masturbation to make me feel better.

Eventually, I had little shame or restraint for my urges. I didn't hesitate to tell friends, or sometimes even strangers, about how great my sex life was — with myself! I showed no restraint.

At the very height of my obsession, I literally could not go without masturbating. It was no longer done solely for fun and feeling good. I *had to* do it. Once a day was rarely enough. I could not imagine ever stopping.

If you saw me today, it may seem like I took some pretty drastic measures to try to stop my habit. You see, I accidentally injured my spinal cord shortly after graduating high school, and I've been unable to move or feel my body since. Obviously, paralysis was not one of the dreams I had for my life, but at least my masturbation issues should have been easily solved, right?

Wrong.

I quickly learned how much of an incredible role the mind plays in sexual experience.

My mind remained deeply entrenched with my obsession with masturbation. Granted, "imagining touch" did not feel quite the same. I won't pretend that paralysis had no effect, but I still looked forward to experiencing any sexual pleasure I could — even if only in my mind. My injury clearly did not paralyze my imagination and fantasies.

The freedom I never expected — or even knew I wanted — eventually came after more than a year of being paralyzed. It didn't happen because I finally became too frustrated with paralysis. It happened because of Jesus. His reality shook me hard, and His love was beyond any of my wildest imaginations. There's not enough space to tell how God radically changed my heart and delivered me from many areas of darkness and addiction. I can only assure you that God's complete awesomeness brought freedom to this slave.

As a new Christian, I began the journey of living out the freedom God desired for me. My deepest areas of bondage would not easily release me. Regarding masturbation specifically, temptation overwhelmed me at times. Nighttime was the most difficult. With defenses down as sleep and dreams approached, it was as if my mind knew no response aside from indulging whatever unwanted fantasies had aroused.

I thought there must have been something wrong with me to continue feeling "turned on" so often. Talking to God about this was difficult. Talking to others was out of the question, at least initially.

Perhaps partly out of some attempt to ease my shame and partly out of extreme exasperation, I began to question what God thought about masturbation. I realized that the Bible never mentions it. Maybe it wasn't so bad? Maybe I was making too much of it and felt needlessly ashamed? On some level, I just wanted masturbation to be okay with God. That would be one less struggle for me. However, *more than anything*, I so desperately desired to know and live by whatever was true and would please my Savior.

As I intensely pursued my relationship with Jesus, I began to discover the answers to my questions. The more I got to know Him, the more my passion grew to please Him. As I realized loving others rightly would make Him smile, reducing people to objects of fantasy and lust began to lose much of its appeal. Indulging in perverted imaginations could not be done with a clear conscience. Instead of being controlled by long-standing habits, I began to grow in self-control.

> "Reducing people to objects of fantasy and lust began to lose much of its appeal."

I knew God saw the depths of the fantasies that I was tempted to entertain. While God's holiness was reason enough to keep my heart and mind pure, I realized that God deeply desired the best for me. He knew how my fantasies distorted how I viewed and treated others. He knew how they could bring destruction to future relationships. He knew the loneliness and isolation that accompanied masturbation. He knew the addictive ways that temporary sexual pleasures could banish self-control and take over my life. He saw everything. *He wanted better for me.*

Change came as I simply continued to get to know Jesus and His amazing love and holiness. I'm not sure that any "thou shalt not masturbate" command would have gripped my heart with love to please God in quite the same way. While I realized that the physical act of masturbation is very real and powerful, I also realized (with the aid of paralysis) that it is just as much — if not even more so — an issue of the heart and mind.

Be brutally honest with God.

God was gentle yet persistent in showing me how so much of what accompanied masturbation both breaks His heart and simultaneously perpetuates my own brokenness. Fantasy, lust, and lack of self-control not only distanced me from God, but from others as well. They distorted the best that God wanted for me.

Freedom came.

I had to learn to choose to listen to God's call to me over the incessant screams of my old ways. My mind pleaded for touch. But thankfully, as hard as it was, saying no became easier over time.

I must admit, though, that there were times I said yes and gave in. Fear, shame, and discouragement left me wanting to hide from God. I felt so disgusting and could not imagine that He would want me. Yet what was so wonderful and still brings tears to my eyes was the tender understanding that God reached me with. He was not content to leave me cowering. Nothing took Him by surprise. He wanted me to trust Him even with what I considered most shameful.

This is where the freedom journey gets craziest. God gave me a glimpse of just how insanely great His love is. He wanted me to let Him in even more. I wrestled a lot, believing God surely didn't want me to be *that* vulnerable with Him! Yet, as I risked learning how to be brutally honest as I talked with God, He began to powerfully break the holds of my shame and isolation. At first, returning to God *after* the times I had said yes to temptation was challenging enough. But God began to show me how deeply He wished for me to welcome Him into my struggle completely — *during* the hardest times, not just after.

Eventually, I began to open all of my heart for God to access completely. I began to welcome Him into my moments of temptation. I had to fight through the embarrassment I felt in front of such a holy God, but He continued to show His amazing compassion. It was here I learned that feeling arousal *itself* was not bad — God designed it! I had felt needlessly ashamed of some things for too long.

I learned that it was what I decided to do next with feelings of arousal that mattered the most. Instead, I began to tell God what I was feeling, how I felt tempted, and how I desperately needed His help to choose what pleases Him.

The more honest I learned to be with God in my struggle, the freer I became. Sometimes I would just talk to God until feelings of arousal went away. I was slowly learning self-control. I was learning to focus on God instead of fantasies. He was always patient and merciful.

Today I marvel at where God has taken me. I never thought that the teenager who filled almost every moment alone with masturbation would find freedom and actually enjoy peaceful moments alone with God. Perhaps I never would have known how much God desires the best for not only my body, but also my heart, mind, soul, and relationships.

The more I see God's love, the greater my desire is to please Him instead of myself. Gratefully, moments of temptation have become far less frequent than I ever thought possible. I have found that during some of the most inconvenient and extremely stressful times in my life, the desire to masturbate can be quite overwhelming. But God has helped me learn to anticipate this struggle when stressed and discover new ways to cope. He remains faithfully by my side — no matter what.

Masturbation may always be an area of struggle for me. Or perhaps I'll look back in several years and realize that I no longer know what masturbation is like. Either way, I know that masturbation no longer has control over me. I have a new Master. He continues to break the grips of shame. Just sharing about this struggle is a huge testimony to God's work!

I no longer pridefully boast as I did in high school or share as a comedian hoping to draw some laughs. I'm hopeful that my story might also help other girls with similar struggles feel less alone. Yet even more than this, I wish to be a witness to the freedom that is possible through God's amazing love.

As I journey onward, I know God has me covered. Jesus is so much bigger than any of my struggles. Masturbation doesn't scare Him. Remaining honest and vulnerable is worth it. He is trustworthy in brokenness. Striving to love and please such a great God with all my heart, mind, and soul is my greatest honor. No other pleasure can compare.

* * *

Jessica's story is brutally honest — she admits masturbation didn't start out as a huge issue for her. It started out as something she enjoyed, something she controlled. And some of the girls I talk with can relate. It's better than real sex, they say, because they aren't risking getting pregnant, they won't get STDs, and there's nothing specific in the Bible that says they shouldn't do it.

I'm not writing this chapter to argue any of those points. I'm writing this chapter for the girls who, like Jessica, feel out of control. I'm writing for the girls who know the loneliness and isolation firsthand. I'm writing for the girls whose masturbation is no longer a means of "saving themselves" but instead a trap that has ensnared them into porn and obsessive sexual behaviors. If this isn't you — be thankful. And move on to the next chapter.[3]

For everyone who's still with me, admitting you have a problem is only the first step. (After all, you wouldn't get in the car to go

---

3. Unless you have a friend whose struggles you'd like to understand.

somewhere and simply start it. You actually have to accelerate to get anywhere.)

I'm not a psychologist, and I've never struggled with masturbation. But I am a journalist, and I know how to ask people questions. So that's what I did. These are a few tips people who have struggled with masturbation wanted to share with you:

- Talk with a professional, preferably a Christian counselor trained to help with this issue.
- Avoid the places that make you want to masturbate.
- Try to get to the root of the problem — what emotional need inside of you caused you to turn to masturbation? Again, a counselor can help you delve into this.
- Avoid looking at pornography or television shows that make you want to masturbate.
- Get outside when temptations come. Go somewhere public or hang out with friends to get your mind off things.
- Talk with God about it. Be blatantly honest. He can handle it.
- Have reasonable expectations. If you fail, talk with someone who can help you get at the core cause for why you're struggling and form a plan to stop.
- Realize you're not alone. People get into tough situations all the time. Don't believe me? Just read the next section.

Lighten Up: You're Not Alone

I promised I wouldn't tell any awkward or immature jokes to make my point in this chapter. But I didn't promise I wouldn't tell any awkward or immature stories.[4]

---

4. After all, this chapter wouldn't be complete if I didn't make fun of myself at least once. It will make you feel better. I promise.

A few years ago,[5] when I was working for a teen ministry, I found myself in an odd situation. My boss said, "I'm leaving — I need you to perform a job interview."

And I said, "But I don't know how."

And he said, "Okay, perform it anyway."

And he walked out the door.

First of all, I was tired. Second of all, I was crabby. Third of all, I had to figure out whether our ministry should hire this gangly, tall, insanely smart rocket scientist[6] to help us babysit kids for the summer.

I invited the dude to sit down as I looked over his background check. Darn it — clean. No reason to cut the interview. So now it was all about the soul-searching questions like "Do you have a death wish since want to work with these kids?" and "Does $6.50 an hour sound okay to you?"

I eased into the chair. Awkward silence. The rocket scientist looked as nervous as I felt.[7]

"So," I said as I leaned back in my chair, "d-d-d-d-d-d-d — "

And that's all I got out.

Because, before I knew it, my head was making contact with the floor. My shoe was flying through the air straight for my boss's window. And the rocket scientist was, well, staring. (Apparently, the skirt I'd chosen for the day was a little more revealing when gaping open and displaying my underwear.)[8]

I wish I was making this story up.

There may not be a happy ending, but there is a moral. It goes like this: Life is going to be embarrassing sometimes. You may feel shy about the fact that you struggle with masturbation. But friend,

---

5. B.E. — Before Ethan
6. I'm not kidding! He was going to be a rocket scientist when he finished school!
7. College is apparently expensive for rocket-scientists-to-be. He needed this paycheck.
8. They were red. And I'm pretty sure by Jewish law the rocket scientist would have had to marry me.

you are not alone. No one is going to look down on you if you'll just acknowledge what's going on and ask for help.

There is also a second moral to the story, and that is that when you are willing to get past the embarrassment, lasting friendships might result.

That rocket scientist dude? Yeah, we laughed pretty hard before he helped me up off the floor. Also, we're still friends. And anytime he wants to dig up dirt on me, he doesn't have to look far.[9]

(UN)SCIENTIFIC QUIZ

How Good Are You at Asking for Help?

1. You're carrying groceries to your mom's car. A cute guy asks to help. You:
   a. Melt into a pile of mush and ask him to marry you.
   b. Give him your best death stare.
   c. Say okay; you don't want to drop the spaghetti sauce.

2. You've been feeling a little depressed lately. You:
   a. Post about it on Facebook and wait for the replies to pour in.
   b. Steel yourself and deal with it.
   c. Ask someone you trust to listen to what's going on in your heart.

3. Your parents are getting a divorce. You:
   a. Tell everyone you see, from the bus-stop crowd to the janitor.
   b. Write in your diary.
   c. Ask your youth leader if she has time to listen.

------

9. Except for the fact that he has nothing on me now that I've published this story for all the world to see.

4. You're painting your room. You:
   a. Post a sign-up list at school for painter assistants.
   b. Do it yourself, even though it takes six days.
   c. Offer free food to any of your friends who will lend a hand.

BARE NAKED RESULTS

Mostly a's: You're pretty good at asking for help, but you might want to be a little more selective about whom you share your problems with. You don't need to tell everyone — just the select people who might be able to help.

Mostly b's: You're pretty quiet and independent. It wouldn't hurt to open up a little and ask for help when you need it.

Mostly c's: Your approach is well-balanced. You're not afraid to ask for help, but you're not blabbering your problems to everyone either. Nice work!

BARE NAKED JOURNAL

What types of questions has this chapter brought up in your heart?

_____

_____

_____

Where can you go to pursue answers to those heart questions?

_____

_____

_____

What are some ways you can reach out to others who are struggling with the questions in this chapter?

_____

_____

_____

LIE #8

I Need a Guy to Help Me Feel Complete

THERE'S SOMETHING ABOUT BEING drunk at a Bible study that turns heads. I didn't mean for it to happen, but it did.

My new friend Glenda, who'd talked me into this Bible study thing in the first place, abandoned me in favor of the bathroom.

It was about this time that I started to get nervous. See, I may be a barrel of laughs on paper, but put me in front of a crowd and I clam up faster than a dead parrot. And, boy, was there a crowd. As far as my eyes could see, strangers lined up in chairs across the living room, all laughing and talking.[1]

Suddenly, the brilliant idea hit me: I could do this. I could blend

---

1. The people were laughing and talking, not the chairs.

in. I'd be so quiet, so serene, so invisible that no one would even try to carry on a conversation with me. And what better way to do that than to hide in the back row?

I began my trek to the back of the room and breathed a mental sigh of relief. I was halfway, and no one had even looked at me. My plan was working. I'd just walk to the back corner, climb over a few metal folding chairs, and ...

Then it happened.

I was attacked.[2] I felt myself fall in slow motion — first my nose, then my butt, then my knees slamming into the carpet. My spine played a game of Twister with the chair and lost. Badly.

Maybe no one will notice I'm eating carpet ...

Then I heard it: the chair crashing into the chair next to it. And the chair next to it. And the chair next to it.

There is no subtle way to disguise the sound of a metal avalanche. As the seats clanged one after the other, the rest of the room went deadly quiet. No laughter. No talking. Only wide-eyed stares.

Being a master of words, I, of course, thought of something brilliant to say. "I ... ummm ... the chair ..." It was then that I realized there was something wet on my face. Blood? My finger touched the corner of my mouth.

Drool.

Apparently, my head hit the floor a little harder than I realized. Every word of explanation I tried to utter came out as a jumbled, slurred mess.[3] To all the world, it would appear I was drunk. At a Bible study — which only made me more speechless.

BaRe NaKeD tip

Things are not always what they appear to be.

---

2. By a folding chair.
3. I'm pretty sure I had flashbacks to speech class.

I heard there were a lot of rumors after that night. Apparently, people made a lot of assumptions about me. And rightly so. Every piece of evidence pointed to me being intoxicated. Why wouldn't Christians talk about it?

That's what humans do. We take the facts and, using sound reasoning, arrive at a conclusion. We calculate what other people say (and, boy, do people like to talk about "drunks" at Bible studies), and we tally the results. Then we make decisions based on those results.

But what if those results are actually well-disguised lies?

I can't blame the Bible study people for believing the lie. I make decisions based on lies all the time. I buy beauty products, watch sitcoms, and choose friends — all based on my assumptions.[4] But I've believed dangerous lies in my lifetime. Lies like *there's something missing in my life, and I need someone to complete it.*

Okay, so that's not a total lie. See, Satan is the master of half-lies. He'll take a truth — like the fact that *there's something missing in my life* — and he'll add a lie — like *I need someone to complete it.*

But the word *someone* is just so vague. I could fill that space with anyone or anything. At least I could try to. Just like a woman named Oneal Morris allegedly tried to fill a woman's butt cheeks with a substance called Fix-A-Flat.[a]

Filling the Void

I'm not gonna lie — when I read the story about Oneal, it sounded like a cheap solution to my own problem. See, there are things I'd like to improve about myself.[5] (You can stop reading now, Mom, 'cause this is gonna get ugly.)

---

4. Do the words "perfectly shaped eyebrows" mean anything to you?
5. Here's where, for the sake of my mother, I mention stuff like my character, my love for others, and my concern for the poor.

I am one of millions of Americans who suffer from something called NBS (No Butt Syndrome). I know this because I was flipping through the panty rack at the store the other day and pulled out what appeared to be a padded bra in the wrong section. Imagine my amazement when I realized it was underwear — with butt implants.

My heart leaped. I was not alone.

What I didn't realize was that there was Oneal's at-home, minimal-cost, permanent solution for this dilemma: injecting myself with items like cement, "Fix-A-Flat," mineral oil, and superglue.[6] At least, that's what a Florida woman thought when she allegedly allowed Oneal Morris to do just that to her, which resulted in a trip to the hospital and a lot of surgeries and apparently a much smaller butt than she started with.

You see my point. When you have a void to fill, not just any filling will do.

The Void in Our Hearts

This is where the butt analogy ends, because otherwise it just gets awkward. Instead, I want to get real with you. I want to get bare about my past. I want to tell you things I've never told anyone except my best friend, Ethan.

I am needy.

There you have it. But this confession goes much deeper than just a little neediness. It goes into the emptiness that every living, breathing human being feels at one time or another. It's the ache that comes when we're by ourselves, lying in bed all alone.

None of us likes to talk about it, and if we're really good, we can even hide it from ourselves. We only feel it for one second before we pick up the phone and text someone, log on to Facebook, or finally

---

6. Don't try this at home. Seriously.

drift off to sleep. Most of the time we don't even think about it, but deep down we know there's something missing.

Can I say something? There is no shame in this void. The maker of the world said, "It is not good for … man [or woman] to be alone" (Genesis 2:18). He made us with this hole in our hearts to be filled by Him, but sometimes things happen that make this hole even deeper. So we deny it — just like my friend Betsy did.

SPOTLIGHT
Author Betsy St. Amant

You know 'em — the girls who are never single, who change boyfriends faster than they change their nail polish, who keep a guy at their side like they would a Chihuahua in a designer handbag. Those girls are easy to judge, easy to smirk at and think, "I'd never be like that. I don't need a guy to complete me."

But then your long-term boyfriend breaks up with you, the guy you thought you'd be with forever, and you're left thinking, "Now what?"

I was that girl once.

My heart was broken by a guy who used words like *love* and *forever* and then disappeared quicker than a guy running from a *Twilight* preview. His reason? "I don't think it's God's will for us to be together."

Umm … okay.

I was suddenly eighteen and alone, for the first time in my entire dating life. I never realized that I'd gone from boyfriend to boyfriend just like all those girls I criticized. The difference was I was more subtle about it — so much so that I hadn't ever seen it for myself. I thought it was different my relationships lasted months or years. But the concept was the same — somewhere in the back of my mind, I'd come to believe I needed a guy to be whole, to matter, to be worth something.

When I saw all of this happening, I fought a lot of guilt, because even though I finally saw the truth, it didn't really change anything. I *wanted* a boyfriend. I wanted to be wanted. I needed to be wanted.

And what did that say about my relationship with God?

It was finally time to come to terms with myself and with my Creator. The one who wanted me to want Him more than a boyfriend. Who wanted me to sit at His feet more than He wanted me to sit in a church pew holding hands with a new guy. Who wanted me to spend time in His Word more than He wanted me to obsess over text messages from a BF.

So I spent some time with just Him and me.

You know what? My ex-boyfriend was right. It wasn't God's will for us to be together, because you know what happened? As soon as I truly convinced my heart that I didn't need a boyfriend, and I was okay with it, my future husband strolled up to the front door of my parents' house wearing a cowboy hat and offering to mow the yard. (He also had a gallon of mint chocolate chip ice cream under one arm to help ease the just-got-my-wisdom-teeth-out pain I was in.) *That* was God's will.

And while my husband doesn't complete me, he did complete God's plan for me in that area of my life.

Now I see the difference.

* * *

BARE NAKED QUOTE

"Anytime a girl was single for more than a few months or a year, she was instantly thrown into the 'rejection' pile with very little hope of getting out. It was kind of like quicksand — no matter how much she thrashed, she would just find herself sinking down deeper."

– Author Alex Schnee

Your story is different from Betsy's It may not be as dramatic, but your void may run just as deep. Maybe your parents split. Maybe you witnessed violence. Maybe you experienced abuse. Maybe the bully wouldn't leave you alone. Maybe someone you loved walked away. The pain created the void.

Your pain doesn't have to be on this list for you to understand the void that life can leave. Sometimes when you are alone, the darkness envelops you. You feel hollow — empty — and needy. And when someone comes along who seems to fill that void, why not take him up on it? I did.

In Walks the Hero

"Stay away from him."

Well, you can't say my sister didn't warn me. But I mean, really. He was just a friend. And he cared about me.

"He's a creep."

There went Miss Drama again. If my friend was a creep, why would he tell me over and over again that he didn't want anything from me? That he just wanted to be friends? That I was like a daughter to him?

The phone calls grew more frequent and later into the night. When he listened, I knew someone cared. Little by little, the door to my heart began to open, and I told him things I hadn't told anyone. Little by little, I grew attached to this man who became one of the best friends I'd ever had.

Turns out he wanted more.

I'll give the man the benefit of the doubt. The friendship probably didn't start out this way for him — he probably really did just want to know me. But the fact is, because of my neediness — because I didn't know where to go with the emptiness I felt inside — I allowed myself to become emotionally dependent on our friendship. As this man and I grew closer, the natural reaction for him was to want things to become romantic. After all, I was single and so was he. But I was sixteen, and he was forty — not exactly appropriate.

Girls, when he told me he was interested in me romantically, I knew it was time to turn and run. But in the end, when I did run, I felt the deep heartache of losing one of my best friends, even though I did not feel the same romance he felt for me. I'd turned to a place that wasn't safe for me emotionally, and I ended up feeling emptier inside than I'd ever felt. Later, I discovered what my friend Susie learned after years of living the single life. But I won't tell you — I'll let her do that.

SPOTLIGHT
Susie Shellenberger, Editor, Sisterhood Magazine

Yes, I know God wired us to desire relationships. And it's totally normal to *want* a guy. But to believe a guy will make me complete? Nothing could be further from the truth.

I've discovered that my security, my wholeness, and my self-worth will never come from another person. Those things can only be found in a tight, growing, intimate relationship with Christ.

I'd love to be married — and God is certainly *big* enough to bring the right man into my life at just the right time — but until then I've learned to be at peace trusting Christ with my singleness.

I've also decided to live life to the max! The apostle Paul suggests in 1 Corinthians 7:32 – 35 that being single can give us more opportunities to serve Christ. I like that. So I'm taking advantage of it.

Years ago I decided to launch an annual two-week international summer missions trip for teen guys and girls. I've been able to take nearly eight thousand teens on mission trips to Bolivia, Costa Rica,

Panama, Venezuela, Brazil, Peru, Guatemala, and Ecuador. If I were married, I may not have had the opportunity to engage so fully in this.

Being single leaves lots of room for adventures.

I've also determined to turn personal vacations into ministry adventures, and always take a friend with me to enjoy the escapade. I've stood on the Great Wall of China, snorkeled the Great Barrier Reef in Australia, spent the night in primitive huts and villages in Burma, and visited the Kiri Kiri tribe (who are still living as if it's the Stone Age) an area so remote in Irian Jaya that few have even heard of it.

I've been to every continent in the world (yes, even Antarctica) and have had the privilege of hanging out with missionary kids and speaking in chapel at their schools in several African countries, prayed with teen prostitutes, hung out in a leper colony in India, rode elephants in Thailand, rode camels in China, shopped for pearls in Japan, got custom-made clothing in Singapore, and on and on.

If I were married, would I still be able to have the adventurous life I'm enjoying? I'm guessing if I were married, my priorities would change. I think I'd want to spend more time at home, because my desire would be to nurture my husband and to be the best wife possible. I wouldn't be as free to pick up and go wherever, whenever, and do whatever for God, because I'd have responsibilities at home.

I often wonder, *Will I get married?*

I don't know the answer.

But I *do* know that I can trust God with it. And that takes away all the pressure! See, whenever I meet a single guy, I don't have to start thinking, *Do I look okay? Is he the one? Should I make a move?* I can simply relax, knowing God is in charge of my life. If He wants me married,

He's certainly powerful enough to orchestrate that without me having to jump in and try to make things happen.

And meanwhile? I will continue to travel the world, disciple girls, and speak to audiences about developing intimacy with Christ — and I'll continue to live in total joy!

My life is full.

My life is exciting.

And it's all because I'm *complete* in Christ alone.

✳ ✳ ✳

I'm not gonna lie — some of the things Susie's singleness allows her to do are amazing. But even if you can't shop for pearls or pray with prostitutes, there are so many things you *can* do that I, Mrs. Married, *sometimes miss.*

1. I would love to work out again. Picking up a toddler doesn't count.
2. Going back to school would be *amazing*. You have time to plan or change your career — anything is possible at this phase in your life!
3. I wish I had time to volunteer things again, like spending more time with underprivileged kids, or cheering someone up at the old folks' home.
4. Last — but most important — now is the perfect time to find out who you are in God's eyes. To become secure in the opinion of you that never changes. Take this opportunity to know him — it is something you won't regret!

If I'd known Jesus in that deep way I'm talking about — if I'd known that I didn't *need anyone but him to be* complete — I could have avoided the heartache of depending on someone else emotionally. My older friend I told you about earlier wasn't the only guy

I depended on. There were others. Time and time again (before I met Ethan), I found myself drawn to boys I thought would meet my needs. Time and time again, I discovered that those guys disappointed me. Eventually, I realized I was expecting something that wasn't fair for them — I was expecting them to fill the emotional void only one other person could fill.

Jesus.

If This Sounds Too Easy, Keep Reading

This may sound like a pat answer to you: *Connect* with God and get your needs met. You've heard it before — God is the well of love that won't run dry. But if connecting to God worked, why aren't more people doing it? Why are so many of us going from relationship to relationship? Why are so many of us still feeling empty?

BaRe NaKeD tip

Building relationships takes time — even building a relationship with God.

To answer this, I need to ask you a question: Do you remember at the beginning of the chapter when we talked about the assumptions the Bible study people made about me? Well, it turns out our hearts do the same thing about God. Just like the Bible study people's assumptions, ours aren't intentional. They just sort of sneak in. And they keep us from experiencing God's love in a life-altering way.

For instance, when the man I cared about as a friend decided he wanted romance, my natural reaction was to ask why God allowed it. After all, wasn't he in control of the situation? Why would he allow this to happen in the first place?

There was nothing wrong with asking those questions — in fact, I believe God likes honest questions.[7] The problem is when those questions go unanswered. Little by little, lies creep in and begin to block out the one person who can help us.

This is exactly what our enemy Satan wants. The Bible says Satan has come to steal, kill, and destroy. But God has come to give us life — love — abundantly (John 10:10). The question is, will we let the Life-giver change our assumptions?

How God Met Me ... How He Wants to Meet You

I lay on the floor, hot tears rolling down my cheeks. I was fourteen years old. *I can't do this anymore, God. I can't keep going.*

Alone.

Four years before, I'd stood at the edge of the pool during swim practice, toes barely touching the water. I wasn't thinking about the strange smell, I wasn't thinking about the headache, I wasn't thinking about anything except my form as I dove ...

My face hit the water and my brain knew immediately that something was wrong. My eyes burned and my lungs tried to inhale as I came up for air. I could tell the chlorine content was high, but it didn't seem that much higher than the day before. And the pool was full of people that day — surely it was safe to swim. I put one arm in front of the other until I was done — fifteen laps later. It was a decision I would regret for the next ten years.

It didn't take long for my body to react to what I later learned was an excessively high chlorine level; the pool filter was broken, yet the management continued to dump massive amounts of chemicals into the water. Since I didn't know about the problem, I continued to swim day after day for weeks — causing my immune system to

---

7. Look at the Psalms if you don't believe me.

break down and my body to succumb to an infection that would leave me bedridden for many of the next ten years.

I don't tell you this story to make you feel sorry for me. I don't bare my heart because I need your sympathy. I tell you this because I want you to know that I understand what it's like to feel out of control. I understand what it's like to feel helpless. I understand what it's like to think no one understands what you're going through. And I understand what it's like to try to fix things on your own.

I thought I would be better by now. I thought that one day, after all the prayers my friends and I could muster, I would wake up whole.

That day didn't come.

My friends were tired of waiting. One by one they stopped calling, stopped visiting, stopped remembering.

God, if You're there, give me one reason to stay here. One reason to keep breathing.

I stared at the wall — not expecting an answer. Then I saw it. On my bulletin board was a card from a church lady that said, "He who dwells in the secret place of the Most High shall abide in the shadow of the Almighty."

The sobs escaped from somewhere deep inside of me.

I don't know where that secret place is, but God, I want to be there.

Something changed in that moment. I wish I could say that magically my friends started calling or that my body was miraculously healed. But the change was deeper. For the first time, I could see Jesus, carrying me like a wounded sheep, close to His heart. I could see His tears, His agony, His pain for me.

It was six more years before the Gentle Shepherd chose to heal my body. I still had days when I was angry, days when I couldn't feel His presence, days when I wanted to end it all. But in those desperate moments, I reached out for that secret place. I asked Jesus to meet me there.

I don't know what you're going through — I don't know what made your void so deep — but I want you to know you have a Gentle Shepherd, a healer of the deepest parts of you. And I want you to know that He longs to hold you close to His heart. He wants to be near you in that secret place.

Would you ask Him to do that for you today? Would you ask Him to help you seek Him? Here are some words that might help you along when you talk to Him:

Jesus, I lay down my assumptions about You. Please meet me where I am — in the midst of my emptiness — and begin to fill my void. I allow my heart to open to You and ask You to enter the deepest parts of it to make me whole. In Jesus's name. Amen.

But I'm Not Comfortable with Jesus

Recently, I was reminded of a little girl I worked with at summer camp. Sarah had been terribly abused, and she wouldn't let anyone come near her. When all the kids crowded around me at night and begged for hugs, she stayed in the corner with her arms crossed. It wasn't okay for her to come close. It wasn't safe.

That's how I felt with Jesus for a long time. Maybe you can relate. For years I had this strong desire to let Him hold me, to comfort me — but he wasn't safe. He let bad things happen to me, and even though I wanted to forgive Him, even though I knew deep down it wasn't His fault, I couldn't seem to get close to Him.

Then I asked Him to show me how He felt when I was hurting all alone. In my mind's eye, I saw a little dog who had been abused. The dog couldn't trust anyone. It was cornered, trembling, and scared. Jesus wanted to come close to the dog, but He knew it needed time to heal. The dog was scared of people in general and thought everyone wanted to mistreat it.

I realized I was just like that dog. Jesus knew I needed time. And just like the little girl at summer camp, it was okay that I didn't want a good-night hug. It was okay that I needed to sit in the corner with my arms crossed for a little while. Even if it took the rest of my life, He wasn't going to force himself on me.

Then one night I found myself sitting in His lap. I didn't expect it. And I realized it was okay. He hadn't put me there. Little by little, I'd inched up to Him until it was safe. And when I saw his caring, loving eyes, I knew He wouldn't hurt me. I knew He had only good, pure intentions toward me.

Sometimes I still get scared. Sometimes I'm not ready to sit in His lap. Sometimes he's not the first place I run. But then I remember Sarah. I remember the day we stood by the swimming pool. I remember her big brown eyes when she asked, "Would you help me swim?"

"Are you sure?" I asked, uncertain. Would she really be okay if I held her?

"Yeah." She smiled. "Hold me up while I flap my arms around …"

I taught Sarah to swim that day. She flapped her arms in the shallow water while my hands held her steady. Even her eyes smiled.

Sarah wasn't "cured" after that experience. She was still shy and scared at times. But gradually she began to understand that I did not want to hurt her. Eventually, as our relationship built over the years after summer camp (Sarah is now seventeen!), she began to believe that I was trustworthy.

Relationships take time. God does want to feel trustworthy to you. He wants to be the one to fill you up with love, but it's not going to happen overnight. He doesn't want to scare you. He doesn't want to force himself on you. It's okay if you're not ready to climb up into His lap just yet. It's okay if your trust in Him is still building (I know mine is).

But God does want you to be safe. He wants to help you stop walking into unhealthy relationships to meet your emotional needs. Maybe you're not in a place just yet where you can run to Him for your love. But you can surround yourself with people — safe people — who can help Him meet your needs.

Here's an example of what a safe person vs. an unsafe person might look like:

An unsafe person ...	A safe person ...
Recently became a Christian	Has known Christ for some time
Has all the answers herself	Helps you connect with God for the answers
Is a guy	Is a woman
Tells you how to solve your problem	Cares about how you feel while helping you with the problem
Is moody and unstable	Has emotional health in her other relationships
Is close to your age	Has years of life experience to help guide you

Where to Find a Safe Person

"We're all just selfish pigs, and that's why God allows us to suffer."

I felt my breath catch in my throat. Was this woman serious? I'd just been honest with her about how things were going — I thought she wanted to know since she'd asked — and this is what she told me? That I was a selfish pig?

Sadly, you may have experienced something similar. Like me, you may have discovered that church isn't always as safe as God designed it to be. In your search for someone to talk to, you may have run across people who just don't get it. They appear to be safe on the outside, but the more you trust them the more you discover they're not the help you hoped they'd be.

Please don't let these bad experiences stop you from reaching out. For every unsafe person you've met, there is someone safe out there for you to talk to. If you really can't think of anyone, it probably wouldn't hurt to look into meeting with a Christian counselor. If you don't like the one you meet first, keep looking until you find someone who can help you with the void inside.

The Haunted House

I'd never seen anything like it. The roof was caved. The front door was busted. The yard was an African safari gone bad. My pulse raced as I crept through the tall grass toward the front steps.

Was I out of my mind when I agreed to deliver magazine subscriptions for my brother? Had he forgotten to mention basic details of the job, like the 99 percent probability of death?

I searched the delivery list for the name of the magazine to deliver. *ESPN the Magazine*? *Pure PC*? Anything that involved sitting in front of the TV and ignoring the daylight as it peeked through the roof?

My mind reeled when I saw the title. The list had to be wrong. Was it a typo? The homeowner had ordered — *Better Homes and Gardens.*

Yeah right. She must be dreaming. There was no way this house would ever have fountains, flowers, or anything except a natural skylight after the next rainstorm. I dropped the magazine and ran, huffing and puffing and whispering a prayer of thanks to heaven for a second chance at life.

No ferocious dogs jumped at me. No bugs crawled up my legs.

No creepy old woman chased me over the hedge. In fact, I never saw the woman who lived in that house.

It's been a long time since that scary day. I still drive past the place sometimes (but only on nights when the moon is full and the car is able to go at least ninety-five miles per hour). The house looks worse than ever. The sheets in the windows and the rusting car in the driveway make it appear that the same homeowner still lives there.

I wonder about that person.

I wonder what makes her tick. Is she disabled? Unable to work? Unable to renovate the house but dreaming about it in spite of that? (Or was the magazine a gift from a not-so-subtle neighbor?)

As I wonder about these things, I realize I had a dream too. A dream to renovate my heart. To fill the void inside of me. But it was only a dream. I thought about it a lot. I thought about fixing things up, but I didn't even know where to begin. I was too busy tripping over chairs at Bible studies to connect with the God of the Bible, to allow him to fill me up inside. Instead, I ran to guy after guy in hopes that maybe — just maybe — I wouldn't feel so alone. So empty. Having relationships made me feel like I had worth.

Please don't make the same mistake I did. Don't waste time just dreaming about fixing up your heart. Pursue that dream. Pursue the God of the universe who wants you to be whole inside. He wants your heart to be a fabulous display of his handiwork. He wants to strip down the curtains and fix the leaky roof. He wants to prove that He is able to heal the girls who are broken inside — even the ones who appear to show up drunk at Bible studies.

(UN)SCIENTIFIC QUIZ

Are You a "Safe" Person?

1. Your best friend tells you a secret. You:
   a. Send out an email asking for prayer for an "anonymous" friend.
   b. Send a text to your other friends during class spilling all the details.
   c. Keep it to yourself and pray like she asks.

2. You read something nasty about a friend on Facebook. You're not sure if it's true, so you:
   a. Repost it and wait for replies.
   b. Ask your other friends in person.
   c. Go to your friend and ask gently.

3. Your little brother wets his bed. You:
   a. Go to his class for show-and-tell, and you show and tell.
   b. Berate him for it.
   c. Offer to help him clean it up.

4. You overhear a phone conversation between your mom and your best friend's mom. You:
   a. Repeat everything to your friend, including the fact that her parents are splitting up.
   b. Put out feelers to see how much your friend knows.
   c. Let it drop.

BARE NAKED RESULTS

Mostly a's: You're a little bit of a jerk. (Sorry — it's the truth.) You have a hard time keeping gossip to yourself and should think about biting your tongue more often.

Mostly b's: You take the middle ground, but you could definitely use some practice on your loyalty skills.

Mostly c's: You are kind and compassionate. You ask yourself how you would feel in another person's situation, which is good, because you never know — it might happen to you someday.

BARE NAKED JOURNAL

What are some things people might use to try to fill the void in their heart?

_____
_____
_____

What are some things you might use to try to fill your void?

_____
_____
_____

What are some things that have made your void deeper?

_____
_____
_____

Name a couple of places you could go to find someone "safe" to talk to.

_____
_____
_____

LIE #9

Drawing Lines Doesn't Help Me Wait

I ONCE WENT HUNTING WITH my good friend Laura.

Now, I know I'm from the South, but you didn't really think I was going to tell you I went full-fledged, camo-wearing, gun-toting hunting, did you? I did go hunting, but it didn't involve creeping through the woods while looking through a rifle scope. It did, however, involve creeping through the woods while peeping through other people's curtains.[1]

Before you go calling the cops on me for being a complete pervert, I can tell you it was innocent peeping. Laura and I were simply looking for a place to spend the night. A place we had supposedly

---

1. No, I did not go to jail for this.

rented for a girls' retreat. A place that looked very small and blurry in the Internet image.

Add the blurry image to the fact that it was pitch-black outside and there were no house numbers, and you have a recipe for a very cold night in the middle of the woods. As we listened to a dog howl in the distance, you can bet Laura and I found the determination to search for the correct cottage. And what better way to do that than the process of elimination?

"Do you think that's it?" Laura whispered as she pointed to an old green house on the hilltop — also without a house number.

"Do you think it's haunted?" I trembled, my heart beating wildly.

"This can't be it," she finally murmured after creeping up the hillside and trying all the doors to the house.[2] "It must be farther up the road."

Newsflash: Some of you are going to think I'm making this next part up. I swear on my bowl of soup that as we headed farther up the road, there was a tree across it.

I watched as Laura got out of the car, picked the tree up with her bare hands, and shoved it off the side of the cliff. At that moment, I knew: Laura was Clark Kent in disguise.

But if she was such a superhuman, how come she couldn't figure out which cabin we'd rented?

It was then that we noticed that somehow in this desolate place, we still had one cell phone bar. Laura's fingers bobbed up and down faster than a synchronized swim team as I prayed for the rental agency to answer our call. We locked the car doors and waited …

Twenty minutes later we were still reaching voicemail. We had two choices: (a) run the heat in the car 'til the gas ran out and we slowly froze to death or (b) take our best guess at which cabin was ours and hope not to walk in on anyone doing anything funky.

---

2. Twice.

Finally, we found a house with an open door. Checking underneath all of the beds, dressers, and couches, we realized that the boogeyman did not live there. We locked the doors behind us.

The guestbook in the kitchen showed that we were in a cabin owned by the correct rental agency — but there was also a card on the table with someone else's name on it. A different guest. This is when Laura informed me, "I don't think the house in the Internet image was red."

"Oh?" I asked, "And do tell, what color was it?"

"Green."

"I see. And we're sitting in a red house right now?"

"That would be correct," said Laura.[3]

Have you ever tried to watch TV in a 30-degree cabin on a stranger's couch? It is very unnerving. Finally, the phone rang. Not knowing what to do, we answered it.

Shock: "We're in the wrong house," Laura said. "Our house is green with stone on the bottom."

"Green?" I said. "No way."

"But that second green house we passed — it has lights on," she said. "Like someone lives there."

Turns out the cottage owners are like Motel 6 — they leave the light on for ya.

We fled the red house for the green house — where the living room was warm and cozy. We were just beginning to get comfortable when we heard footsteps on the front porch.

Nervous sweat dripped from every pore in my body. Some person was on the front porch — and they were going to fry us up and eat us for breakfast. We hadn't even left a trail of crumbs! In all seriousness though, Laura and I looked at each other terrifiedly.[4] We ran for the front door to be sure it was locked. It was.

---

3. Yes, we really do talk like nerds in real life.
4. Which isn't even a word.

As we looked out the window, we saw it.

There — on the porch — looking in the window at us — was the mammoth neighborhood dog. Then he did something neither of us expected. He popped his head through the doggy door and drooled on the floor.

A couch provides a wonderful barricade in a pinch.[5]

I would be lying if I told you we didn't sleep with the light on. I lay awake most of the night, my adrenaline pumping as the dog barked — wishing with all that was inside of me that we'd scoped this place out in the daylight.

Amazing what a little daylight does for a person. And it's true in a metaphorical sense too — light helps us see with our emotional decisions. *By not deciding beforehand what your physical boundaries are, you are choosing to survive in the dark, creeping around trying not to get caught or hurt.* My friends Jenness and Tracy put it another way. I'll let them tell you about the moment of decision:

SPOTLIGHT
Jenness Walker with Tracy Bowen

Have you ever stood in the middle of a store, pressured by friends, stressed by way too many responsibilities, and struggling with a headache brought on by a lack of chocolate, and made a good choice about buying clothes?

Me neither.

You know the purchase I'm talking about: the outfit you try on again in the privacy of your room and groan out loud about because the color makes your skin look like a three-day-old dish rag, and the

---

5. And a person on the couch keeps even 150-pound dogs on the other side of the door.

outfit kind of hangs like one too. Not to mention it cost you two months' worth of babysitting cash — money you were supposed to be saving toward a car.

The dressing room mirror didn't lie to us. We lied to ourselves. The outfit didn't magically change on the way home, but our perspective changed enough for us to make an honest assessment. How much energy could we save ourselves if we were honest about what works for us and what we can afford before we enter the whole shopping experience?

The good thing about a bad purchase is we can take what we purchase back. When our emotions or peer pressure push us into situations in other areas of our lives, like sexual activity during dating, the consequences are far more painful and not so easily fixed.

We tend to think we are above being mastered by our emotions. We give in to the lie that drawing lines in advance about what we will and will not do is foolish. After all, we are too smart to get caught up in the heat of the moment. We are too mature to give in to the urge to please those around us.

The truth is we all know that it is not wise to wait until we are in an intense situation to make decisions. At least, we know that is true for everyone else. We think we are the exception to the rule. We think we are in control.

And we usually are — right up until the moment when we're not.

The beauty of solid boundaries is that they protect us from reaching that point.

* * *

Let's Talk about Boundaries

"But Daniel resolved not to defile himself."
— *Daniel 1:8*

You probably know about Daniel, but for the quick recap — he was a guy in the Bible who was known for standing up for what he believed in, even when it wasn't popular. He refused to do what the King Darius — who had the power to kill him (and tried to do so twice) — asked him to do. Daniel didn't stand up for what was right because he thought it would be fun. He did it because he knew God's design for him would be more fulfilling than going with the crowd. Daniel knew that honoring God would bring the deepest satisfaction.

That's still true for us.

Here's the thing: The secret to Daniel's success was that he didn't decide what to do at the last minute. He chose *beforehand.* He *resolved* before temptation came in order not to *defile* himself (yeah, those are old-fashioned words, I know — but you get the picture). Another version of the Bible says Daniel "purposed in his heart" (KJV).

I believe that if we're going to stick with something, we have to purpose in our hearts beforehand. I say "we" — and you might be saying, "That's easy for you, Bekah. You're married. You have sex all the time."

BaRe NaKeD tip

Ignore the hormones. I repeat: Ignore the raging hormones.

Remember what I told you earlier? Temptation doesn't end when you get married. You will still be attracted to guys; you're not blind. No matter how wonderful and sexy your husband will be, you will still be human. You will have to remember — just like when you were single — that God has created you to be a one-man woman. That his design is to satisfy you with the amazing spouse he's given you. So in this battle you're fighting, the physical and emotional lines you're drawing in your relationships will not only help you now, but they will also help you after you're married.

However — and this is a *big* however — in order to experience God's best for you, you have to *choose* to step into the light. And that involves getting specific about the lines you will draw physically.

Dead Men Tell No Tales

Before I was a writer, I was a vampire. I'm not sure how it happened, but I think it was mostly about the money. My parents said, "You need to stop mooching and pay for your own cell phone," and I said, "What better way to make some money than to suck blood?"[6]

After a few classes, I signed a piece of paper that said I wouldn't draw anyone's blood unnecessarily. Also that I would donate both my lungs to the hospital if I caused any lawsuits. Then a doctor handed me a needle and told me to get to work. (Seriously … that's all it took.)

The job didn't come with much respect, but thankfully I had my friend Kevin to hang out with. He kept things interesting … especially the day he came running into the lab, red in the face and barely able to speak. Finally he calmed down enough to tell me what had happened.

Despite the fact that Kevin knew lots of patients hated people with needles, he was shocked when one of his patients chose to completely ignore him. *You've got to be kidding*, he thought. *I know I'm not always their favorite person, but to act like I don't exist?*

---

6. Unfortunately, I never sparkled in the sunlight.

Kevin banged on the patient's door. Hospital policy—he had to let her know he was there. A soft rap, a loud thump, then little screams of, "Hello, Mrs. Campbell! I'm here to draw your blood!" Eventually Kevin gave up on the verbal warning and flung open the door.

Kev knew the hospital had some pretty sick patients. Seeing them like that day after day was doing crazy things to his head. So when he heard voices in the room, he thought it must be one of two things: his stressed mind or Mrs. Campbell talking in her sleep.

Actually, it was the TV. He flipped the switch and glared at the patient.

"Mrs. Campbell," he said in his most professional tone, "the doctor ordered some lab work."

Nothing.

"I hate to wake you, but your blood's due back at noon."

Nothing.

"It's 11:59."

Nothing.

At that moment, my friend decided to use the four most-dreaded words—words that made most patients run right out of the room. "I have a needle," he said.

Still nothing.

It was then that Kevin realized Mrs. Campbell was a coma patient. It wasn't marked on the paperwork, but he'd dealt with this problem before. He rolled up her sleeve to peek at her ID, and when he did he thought his heart would stop. On the patient's band were two words that made him want to run right out of the room: Death Certificate.

His heart pounded. His hands shook. Sweat came from every pore in his body. Kevin was in the room with a dead person. He'd just yelled at a dead person. And to make matters worse, he'd expected that dead person to answer him.

Maybe this job is getting to me after all, he thought. There was *no way*—no matter how loud he talked—that Mrs. Campbell was ever going to talk back. She was gone. D-E-A-D.

Be willing to die.

I share this strange story because, as freaky and weird as it is, God says we're supposed to be like dead people. Okay, stay with me here. He doesn't say we're supposed to be lying on a hospital bed with a toe tag. He says it in a metaphorical sense.

I'm not making it up. See here? "Count yourselves dead to sin but alive to God in Christ Jesus" (Romans 6:11).

In other words, when we die to ourselves, we willing kill our own desires. We willing set our own boundaries. When temptations come—like when my boyfriend wants me to look at porn—God wants me to be dead to the part of me that says, "Maybe just once." When everyone's talking about sex, I'm tempted to say, "Everyone else is doing it," but God wants me to say, "I need to change the conversation or leave." When my friends make fun of me for how inexperienced I choose to be, God wants me to act like a dead person.

Daniel faced the same thing. Many of the people who had been taken captive with him into a foreign country wanted to fit in with the natives. You couldn't blame them — they'd been through a lot. They'd lost their homes, families, and well, *everything*, when the Babylonian army captured them as slaves. Now they were comfortable and things were almost back to normal. They only wanted to blend into their new home — to carry on with their lives.

But not Daniel.

It's not that he *wanted* to stand out. That's just what happened. He knew his life had come to a decision point: Did he want to be dead to God or dead to his friends? A lot of his friends probably

> **BARE NAKED QUOTE** 💬
>
> "Jesus doesn't just call us to hang out with Him, then do whatever we please. He calls for radical obedience, right down to our sexual choices. To dismiss that, we dismiss Him. The question becomes, how much do you really love Jesus? Or do you love your desires more?"
>
> — *Author Mary DeMuth*

wanted the easy way out. They were probably willing to sacrifice everything in order to blend in.

But Daniel chose to die to himself.

I don't know about you, but dying to myself doesn't sound like much fun. Sometimes I'd rather be a vampire. It would probably be more acceptable to my friends, right? After all, who wants to hang out with a dead person?

Then I remember: being a dead person doesn't mean I have to stink. It doesn't mean I have to shout "Amen!" during math class or "Hallelujah!" on the football field. It doesn't mean I have to stand on a cardboard box in the cafeteria and shake my Bible at people.

Okay, you ask, how is dying *ever* a good choice? Who *wants* to die? No one. Unless it means that they'll have life that lasts forever. Here's what makes this whole dying thing the best choice:

> [Jesus] called the crowd to him along with his disciples and said: "Whoever wants to be my disciple must deny themselves and take up their cross and follow me. For whoever wants to save their life will lose it, but whoever loses their life for me and for the gospel will save it. What good is it for someone to gain the whole world, yet forfeit their soul? Or what can anyone give in exchange for their soul?" (Mark 8:34 – 37).

Daniel's story speaks to me because he saw that there was something at greater risk than temporary pleasure. He saw that by giving up something today, he could gain something forever.

What if we decided our boundaries beforehand? What if we knew where we were going, and why?

So ... How Far Can I Go?

I cannot tell you how many times I have been asked this question. Ladies, ladies, I find the *How far can I go* question a little bit like asking, "Just how often can I roam unarmed through the woods while dogs howl and I peep in other people's windows? How many windows can I peep into before I get shot at or cut into tiny pieces by a maniac?"

You really want me to answer that question? My editors do. And for that reason, I'm going to get *really* specific here. *Bare naked specific.*

But first you need to meet Christine.

Meet Christine

Christine lives with her husband, Steve. They're like me and Ethan — been married for a good five years. But things are far from boring around their house. They still like each other very, very much. So you can imagine Christine's shock when she walked in on Steve making out with another woman.

There they were — plain as day — sitting on the couch in Christine and Steve's living room. Is *sitting* the correct word? The word is probably more like *leaning*. There was some serious tongue action going on. Tongue action Steve would later describe to his friends as "hot."

But *hot* would probably describe Christine more accurately. In fact, the word *incensed* is more like it. This is where Christine used some words I'm not allowed to repeat in a Christian book.

"What is going on here?"

"What's the problem, babe?" Steve asked. "We were just making out. We weren't having sex. We weren't going all the way."

"But you were — "

"Oh, please. It was nothing. I'm just practicing to be a good kisser for you. How will I know how to kiss you best if I don't kiss other women? Don't you want me to be experienced?"

Okay, now place yourself in Christine's shoes. Maybe you already see the correlation. Christine is fictional, but her story happens every day in youth groups across the country. In fact, you might already be a part of it. So let's think ahead — let's ask the question: do you want to continue to be Steve's "other woman"?

How far would you want your future husband to go with someone else? Do you want your future man to constantly be remembering sexual experiences with other women while he's having them with you?

My friend Holley knows firsthand what I'm talking about. She wants to share her real-life story with you:

SPOTLIGHT
Holley Gerth

I recently came across one of my diaries. It's full of hearts drawn around the name of the boy I liked at the time and wistful fantasies about walking down the aisle one day.

When I finally met the[7] love of my life in college, I did walk down that aisle as a virgin. I'll admit that I felt a bit smug about that accomplishment.

But as the years went by, I realized that *the act* isn't the only thing that affects what happens after we say, "I do."

There were make-out sessions I wish I could take back. Casual kisses that gave away small pieces of me in ways I hadn't realized at the time.

---

7. Real

And, most of all, I realized that I was not a virgin when it came to giving away my heart.

I thought drawing lines was only about physical boundaries. *Do this. Don't do that. Walk right up to that line but don't cross it.* I learned to play that game.

But no one told me the most important line I could ever draw was the one around my heart. "Above all else, guard your heart," cautions the ancient wisdom of Proverbs (4:23). And it's true.

BaRe NaKeD tip

It's not all about physical boundaries. It's about emotional ones too.

Every time I gave a bit of my body away, it began with my heart first. And my emotions followed suit. The physical connection between two people is chemically powerful. It literally bonds us to each other: heart, soul, and skin.

I may have saved my virginity for my husband, but I wish I had saved all of my heart too. I experienced painful breakups, bumpy relationships, and wounds to my confidence that could have been avoided if I'd only said, "I'm not only saving my body for my husband, but I'm also not going to fully give away my heart until I know this man is the one God has for me."

And, really, even in marriage the only one we're to fully give our hearts to is God. No one can satisfy all of our needs. When we expect that of a person, we open ourselves up to disappointment and to going into marriage with unrealistic expectations.

You, beautiful girl, have a heart that is worth treasuring. Draw lines around it. Then draw lines around your body too. We guard what is of value, and you are most certainly worth protecting and cherishing until you find the one man who will do the same for the rest of your life.

✳ ✳ ✳

But We're Going to Get Married!

So you and your guy are serious. You're talking about being together forever. I get that. And I hate to sound mean, but I need to be truthful here. What you have may be amazing, but statistics are not on your side. Here they are:

- The chance of a marriage occurring when a woman is under twenty years old lasting ten years is just over fifty percent. (US Department of Health and Human Services 2010)[a]
- In a national survey on marriage, only 22.1 percent of the people surveyed were married to someone they met in high school or before. (Glenn 2005)
- For people who were divorced, 45.7 percent cited marrying too young as one major reason for their divorce. (Glenn 2005)[b]

You may have made all sorts of promises to your guy, and he may have made all sorts of promises to you. You both mean those promises with all your heart, but the fact is you will probably marry someone other than your high school sweetheart.

But let's give your relationship the benefit of the doubt. Let's say you beat the stats (some of my very good friends were high school sweethearts and are still together years later — so it can definitely happen!). It's important for you both to realize that having physical boundaries now will most likely lead to a more fulfilling sex life after marriage.

And that's what we want, isn't it? To have a fulfilling sex life long-term, rather than fulfillment short-term? But what boundaries are we talking about here? I've had friends tell me that everything short of "going all the way" was okay for short-term happiness. These things were all acceptable as long as the couple planned to get married and didn't want to actually have "real" sex beforehand. But the truth? They're all still sex.

John Regier, founder and director of Caring for the Heart Ministries, has counseled thousands of married couples — most of whom have had premarital sex. The following are the deep, deep issues he says couples experience due to sexual relationships outside of marriage:

- Guilt
- Blame
- Conflict with one another
- Rejection by one another
- Lack of sympathy for each other
- Lack of respect for one another
- Distrust/dishonesty
- Loss of communication
- Loss of spiritual interest
- Financial loss
- Inability to respond physically in marriage
- Lack of fulfillment[c]

These consequences tell a story. If that story is true (and if the couples I interviewed for this book are being honest), then it might be worth your time to create a few physical and emotional boundaries for the relationships in your life, even if you haven't created boundaries before. It's worth your while to draw some lines — to purpose in your heart *beforehand* what will keep you from going down the road to sex. Remember, these boundaries are all for a good purpose: saving the most amazing sexual and emotional intimacy for the most important, long-lasting relationship of your life: marriage.

I Can't Tell You What to Do ... But ...

I can tell you that I (like Erynn in Chapter Two) decided I didn't want the memories of kissing a bunch of other guys rolling around in my brain while I made out with my future husband. I realize this is going to sound really naive — because the girls who helped me write this book tell me about the things that are happening in the bathrooms of their schools — but I'm going to be brutally honest here: even though I shared myself emotionally with several guys, I decided to save my first kiss for my fiancé. I waited until I was committed to the man whom I knew wanted to spend the rest of his life with me. And I have not once regretted it.

I tell you all this with the realization that many of you feel my choice was extreme. So hear me out: I'm not saying you need to save your next kiss until engagement or marriage. I am saying I want to help you think through your boundaries logically. Which of your actions are sexual in nature? What turns you on? Just as important, what turns a guy on? And why might it be a good idea to stop doing it?

Here's a chart that will help you decide your own boundaries. Remember to ask yourself what would be okay if you walked in on your future spouse doing it with someone else *after* marriage. (So what makes it okay *before* marriage?)

For each physical action I provide in the left-hand column, you can choose the appropriate box on the right-hand column:

Action	Definitely Okay	Gray Area	Definitely Not Okay
Hands in hair			
French kissing			
Holding hands			
Sitting alone in the dark			
Playful tickling			
Kissing closed-mouth			
Hands under shirt			
Snuggling fully clothed			
Other _____			

Can I challenge you to look at your choices again? Now I want you to take everything from the Gray Area, erase it, and put it under Definitely Not Okay. Because if something is gray, it's probably on the road to sex, and so it needs to be in the Definitely Not Okay column.

Now I have a bigger challenge for you. I challenge you to make a copy of this chart — or write it on a sticky note — and put it someplace where you will see it often.[8] It doesn't have to be visible to others, only to you. You can even use it as a bookmark or put it in the front pocket of your book bag. Every time you see it, your heart will be strengthened. You may even want to add this verse to the page for more encouragement:

> Each of you should learn to control your own body in a way that is holy and honorable, not in passionate lust.
> — *1 Thessalonians 4:4 – 5*

God is awesome, because He wouldn't command us to control our bodies if He didn't give us the power to do it! He tells us we can "walk in the light, as He is in the light" (1 John 1:7). Because of His power and the ability to "purpose in our hearts," we no longer have to creep around in darkness — we can turn on the lights.

(UN)SCIENTIFIC QUIZ

How Good Are You at Drawing Lines?

1. The Brizowskis ask you to babysit again. Last time their delightful child Bobby lit your hair on fire. You:
   a. Tell them sure, no problem — you wanted a haircut anyway. Maybe it will grow back curly.

---

8. In other words, not inside the cover of your math book.

   b. Tell them you're sorry you have other plans. (Does repainting your chipped pinkie toe count?)

   c. Throw rocks at them while they run from your front door.

2. You were volunteered for the Nerd Committee at school. You:

   a. Jump up and down with feigned delight.

   b. Politely decline and decide to ignore the intended jab.

   c. Practice your four-letter words just to be sure you make your message clear.

3. Your boyfriend wants to see a horror movie. You:

   a. Hate horror movies. But you love holding his hand. You go for it.

   b. Tell him you'll be happy to watch a movie — of your choice.

   c. Laugh until he cries.

4. Your best friend wants to go to that restaurant. You know — the one that gave you food poisoning last week. You:

   a. Say sure, why not? You'll just stay away from the sushi.

   b. Explain your situation. She'll understand.

   c. Tell her you would love to — in another lifetime.

BARE NAKED RESULTS

Mostly a's: You're a nice person, but on the verge of pushover. You could use a little practice putting these two letters together: *N-O*.

Mostly b's: You're polite yet firm. You know what you want, but you don't hurt others' feelings in the process of telling them.

Mostly c's: You have a determined personality, and it serves you well. You might want to mix a little sugar with that spice, though.

BARE NAKED JOURNAL

What's the purpose of creating boundaries in your relationships?

_____

_____

_____

Name some people who can help keep you accountable in your boundaries:

_____

_____

_____

Why is light better than darkness?

_____

_____

_____

What are some steps you take when you are tempted to overstep your boundaries?

_____

_____

_____

LIE #10

I Don't Have to Decide Now

I WAS LYING IN BED when I heard the words: "Come out with your hands up."

It's no secret that I'm not a morning person. My guy[1] gets dressed for work, taps me on the forehead, and feels lucky if I grunt anything other than a bad word back. Even my four-month-old hands me a cup of coffee before asking for breakfast.

When Ethan first married me, there was no four-month-old and no reason in my selfish mind for me to get up first thing in the morning. But my selfishness wasn't the only thing that surprised my new husband — so did the fact that the diamond he bought me doubled

---

1. Also known as Mr. Five a.m. Sunshine.

as a weapon when he startled me out of my sleep. He soon discovered that buying me earplugs was his best defense.

I was wearing said earplugs one morning when he left for work. My white noise fan (another mode of his self-defense) was running so loudly that I didn't even hear him close the door. I also didn't hear the crash of glass, the police sirens, or the little old lady next door screaming like a kid in a Halloween horror flick.[2]

Oddly enough, it was my alarm clock that woke me.

"Stupid ..."

I pulled out an earplug, and it was then that I heard it.

"COME OUT WITH YOUR HANDS UP!"

Then it occurred to me: *Where do you go in a second-story apartment when bullets are about to fly?*

I slid into the bathtub and hoped for the best.

A few hours and a few panicked calls to 911 later, I learned the police had cornered a thief in the downstairs apartment. While I was relieved to learn the dude wasn't actually hiding in my closet, it did get me thinking.[3]

The guy could have been in my closet. And thanks to my earplugs, I never would have known.

Despite the fact that I grew up in a crime-ridden town, saw murders on the front page, and was taught street smarts to the point of paranoia by my mother, I'd let my guard slip. I didn't think it could happen to me. I wasn't prepared.

What does this have to do with deciding for purity?

A lot of us are walking through life with our proverbial earplugs in.

---

2. The neighbors later told me about all of it.
3. I was also relieved of other things ... I'll let you use your imagination.

We're so saturated in our sex-crazed culture that our senses are numbed. Things we might have questioned before now don't even register.

But like it did to me, asleep in bed with my earplugs in, life will eventually sneak up on us. And if we're not prepared — if we haven't decided what to do in a tempting situation beforehand — we might as well just kiss our ideals good-bye. Just like Stephanie Morrill, who has this to say about how important it is not to put off this decision:

SPOTLIGHT
Stephanie Morrill

Even at age three, I liked to be as prepared as possible for life's curveballs. My mother loves to tell the story of how the two of us were out running routine errands when I randomly informed her, "Mom, if something happens to you and Daddy, then I'll go live with Aunt Penny and Uncle Lecil. And if something happens to Aunt Penny and Uncle Lecil, then I'll go live with Nana and Papa."

Uncertainty has always made me itchy. Oh, sure, I can be spontaneous. If we're talking about grabbing some ice cream. And we've already eaten dinner. And if this ice cream run is going to happen a couple hours from now …

My constant need for a plan doesn't always work in my favor — I tend to worry and stress about things that never come to pass — but my planning skills *did* serve me well when it came to preparing for sex.

You see, my husband and I began dating our freshman year of high school after meeting at a youth group retreat. "You can't date him yet!" joked one of my adult friends. "He's the guy you're supposed to marry!"

She was afraid — and she wasn't alone in these fears — that starting our relationship at such a young age would screw things up. Indeed, it was a rougher road than I anticipated. We were together seven years before we married. Our years involved a breakup or two, a very long engagement, and a divine amount of self-control.

But my husband and I had decided independently that we were going to save sex for marriage. We didn't do it out of fear — fear of disease, fear of pregnancy, fear of vulnerability. We did it out of faith.

As early as middle school, I saw God's rule of "sex is only for marriage" as evidence that God cared for me. Just like parents make rules about their kids handling knives or using the stove, God made rules about sex. It was for marriage, and that was for my protection.

It was one thing to say as a seventh grader who spent most evenings alone in my room listening to emo music, "I'm gonna trust God and wait!" If I had postponed my decision making until high school, would I have had the same strength to resist temptation as I gazed into Ben's amazing dark eyes?

Waiting was a choice we had to make over and over. Because we had planned ahead, because we had rooted our trust in God's plans rather than the moods of our bodies, it was easier to throw on the brakes in the heat of the moment and make a (spontaneous) ice cream run.

So ... What's the Point?

I'm going to be brutally honest here, ladies. Statistics show that people who sign purity pledges are almost as likely to have premarital sex as those who don't sign pledges.[a] So I could give you a little piece of paper where you sign your name, the date, and your intention to "save" yourself from here on out — but I'm not sure it would do much good.

Unless we add another element.

You see, Satan's goal is to have you forget about this book. Put it back on the shelf and say, *Well, that was a fun read.*[4] Go about

---

4. Or, *Lame-o!*

your daily life at school, work, whatever — and forget that you ever intended to *resolve yourself* before temptation.

Setting a resolution isn't enough. You need to tell someone about what you've resolved. In fact, don't just tell anyone: Tell someone (or more than one person) who will keep you accountable. Someone who will kick your butt if they see you making out with a guy in the parking lot. Someone who will have the guts to ask you, "So how's that purity thing going?" and have the nerve not to accept "pretty good" as an answer.

Let me make this clear: You are giving yourself the motivation. Your "someone" is keeping you accountable.

"But I don't have anyone like that."

Ha! I read your mind didn't I? I took your excuse. Or I'm about to.

There's a whole community of girls at *www.bekahhamrick martin.com* (a website I happen to be involved in — can you tell from the name?) who are waiting to cheer you on. Waiting to ask you the tough questions. Waiting to meet up with you and share their hearts and their worlds and their struggles. Waiting to be real with you. Waiting to help you. Right here. Right now.

SPOTLIGHT
Author T. Suzanne Eller

A guy shows my friend attention and it meets her need.

Right then.

Right there.

But it always leaves my friend empty in the end. And one time it left her pregnant.

"But, Suzie, I didn't mean to do it. It just happened."

Maybe like my sweet friend, a teen marked with destiny and loved by God, you think that good intentions are enough. But if there's a hole

that needs filled up — and all of us have those gaps — when temptation arrives you might find your good intentions have disappeared,
leaving a mess of feelings and desire in their place.

My friend needed a plan.

*I won't date a guy who doesn't love God — not just attending church,
but completely sold out to Him.*

*I understand that even godly guys face temptation, so I won't put
myself — or them — in situations that make it easy to say "yes."*

*I'll fill up on God daily so that I recognize Him as my need meeter,
rather than turn to others to make me feel worthy or wanted.*

What is your plan? God has marked you as His, and the last thing
He desires is for you to get sidetracked from destiny. Whether a guy is
in the picture or not, decide today.

Right now.

Right here.

✳ ✳ ✳

More Than Surviving

We've all seen the TV show *Survivor.* You know — the one where
they dump a bunch of crazies on an island and let them compete to
stay there. Then the last survivor wins a bunch of money. Or something like that.

Well, I have a confession to make: I've never been on a deserted
island. I have, however, been on a deserted mountainside. In fact, I
spent six years on one. Or was it six summers? Yes, that was it. Six
summers that *felt* like six years.

Okay — the mountainside wasn't *completely* deserted. There
were goats, chickens, and children running through the woods. As
their camp counselor, I was running after them. And I was terrified.

Mostly because I'd never been a camp counselor for goats, chickens, or children before.

It would have helped if they'd spoken English. The children, I mean. But no. Moldovan was the language of choice. The kids had only been in the United States for a few months.[5]

"So," my co-counselor Laura said as we listened to the children chatter in their native language. "What do you think they're talking about?"

"They're talking about killing us," I said as my bottom lip trembled. "They're planning to murder us in our sleep."

We held each other and cried.

After a few hours of crying, we finally came to our senses. When was the last time a seven-year-old killed a camp counselor? Besides, we reasoned, anything these kids could do to us would be nothing compared to the agony I'd inflicted on camp staff members in the past. And then, suddenly, I understood why God had sent Moldovan seven-year-olds to kill me in my sleep. The sins of my past! I shuddered.

"Okay, God," I whispered. "The time I put the blue food coloring in the makeup? Yeah. I'm sorry about that."

Isn't there something else? my conscience asked.

"And the time I sewed up the legs on the underwear."

And?

"And the time I put toothpaste in that Oreo cookie."

And?

Five minutes later, I was still rambling.

"Who are you talking to over there?" Laura asked. "Have you lost your mind?"

"I'm saving us from being killed in our sleep," I said. "Shut up or join in."

---

5. The goats were easier to understand.

After we'd finished clearing our consciences, we knew we could die in peace.

"Okay, kids," we said loudly and slowly. "Time for bed!"

The children stared at us blankly. Five minutes later, we gave up talking and resorted to hand motions. Five minutes after that, we gave up hand motions and resorted to dragging the kids up the mountain to the cabin. (Just kidding. No lawsuits, please.)

It didn't take long for us to realize that the children didn't just speak Moldovan. They also spoke English. Especially words like *Butthead!* and *No!* In fact, they introduced us to a few words we'd never tried before.

Laura and I didn't know each other very well before all of this — we'd only spoken a few times. But you'd better believe we knew each other well when the week was over. We knew our survival depended on our strength as a team. We knew we needed each other to make it through.

You probably see where I'm headed with this. We all need each other. Life is a crazy island. It might not be deserted, but sometimes it feels like it. Does anyone understand what we're going through? Does anyone care? Does anyone know the way through this tangled jungle?

Ecclesiastes 4:9 – 10 says, "Two are better than one, because they have a good return for their labor: If either of them falls down, one can help the other up. But pity anyone who falls and has no one to help them up." That's so true. We really do need friends. But do we want just *anyone* navigating the tough questions with us? Or would we rather navigate with someone who's smart — someone who wants more than to survive — someone who wants to thrive?

But no matter how strong the people who have shared their stories in this book are, and no matter how strong your friends are, we can't make this decision to save sex for marriage for you. We want you to make this decision for yourself. We want you to choose God to fill the void you feel, because in the long run your decision is going to free you to enjoy sex the way it's supposed to be. You'll have a life that is free from fear of STDs, unwanted pregnancies, and, most of all, free from the emotional baggage that accompanies sex outside of marriage.

It's up to you. Give it some thought. Give it some prayer. Then, when you're ready, give it your choice.

(UN)SCIENTIFIC QUIZ

Do You Keep Your Promises?

1. You tell your mom you'll catch the bus at seven in the morning. You:
    a. Get yourself outside by 6:30. Just in case the bus is early.
    b. Roll out of bed at 7:01 after hitting the snooze button twice.
    c. Are showered, fed, and dressed by 6:45 ... p.m.

2. You promise not to hang out with that guy your mom hates. You:
    a. Ignore him the next time you see him.
    b. Sit him down and explain why parting is such sweet sorrow.
    c. Don't hang out with the guy ... around your mom.

3. You promise your childhood friend you'll go to the prom with him ... before your crush asks. You:
    a. Sadly decline your crush.
    b. Ask your friend if you can cancel — he can find someone else, right?
    c. Explain to your friend that you won't be able to commit after all.

4. You tell your sister you'll buy her something nice for her birthday. At the last minute you realize you forgot. You:
   a. Rush to the store and pick up that hat she's been wanting — gift wrapped.
   b. Run to the gas station for some candy.
   c. Grab something from your closet she hasn't seen lately — maybe she won't recognize it.

BARE NAKED RESULTS

Mostly a's: You're loyal and you mean what you say. You follow through with your intentions — which is a great quality! Keep up the great work.

Mostly b's: You have good intentions, but you don't always follow through. Don't worry, though — a little practice and you can learn to keep those promises 100 percent.

Mostly c's: Your lack of empathy for others could keep you from being a promise keeper if you're not careful. Try to think of how other people feel before breaking your promises — it might make all the difference in your choices!

BARE NAKED JOURNAL

Write your own commitment to waiting if you feel led. You can see Suzanne's on page 174 for an example. Be as specific as possible so you won't stray from your goal.

_____

_____

_____

Write down the names of three people you can share your commitment with.

_____

_____

_____

Write the motivation for why you're committing or not committing to waiting.

_____

_____

_____

Endnotes

Lie #1: I Have All the Sex Facts

a. Joe S. McIlhaney Jr. MD and Freda McKissic Bush MD. *Hooked: New Science on How Casual Sex is Affecting Our Children* (Northfield Publishing, New Edition, 2008).

b. "Why Wait: The Benefits of Abstinence until Marriage." Bridget Maher, *Family Research Council*, 2008. www.frc.org/get.cfm?i=IS06B01.

c. Ibid.

d. Meg Meeker MD. *Epidemic: How Teen Sex Is Killing Our Kids* (Lifeline, Washington, D.C, 2002).

e. US Department of Health and Human Services: Centers for Disease Control and Prevention. 1994. *Monthly Vital Statistics Report* 42 (12): 18 – 19.

f. "Teenage Sexual Abstinence and Academic Achievement." Robert Rector and Kirk Johnson, the Heritage Foundation, 2005. www.heritage.org/research/reports/2005/10/teenage-sexual-abstinence-and-academic-achievement.

g. "Adverse Childhood Experiences (ACE) Study: Data and Statistics." US Department of Health and Human Service: Center for Disease Control. www.cdc.gov/ace/prevalence.htm

Lie #2: Waiting Is for Wusses

a. *Centers for Disease Control and Prevention. (2002). Youth risk behavior surveillance.*

b. "Just Your Average Gorgeous American Idol," Tram Kim Nguyen, last modified August 1, 2007. www.glamour.com/magazine/2007/08/jordin-sparks

c. "10 Celebrity Virgins Past and Present," Entertainment Wise, last modified June 25, 2008. www.entertainmentwise.com/photos/43459/8/10-Celebrity-Virgins-Past-Present

d. "Lolo Jones Says Remaining a Virgin Is Harder than Training for the Olympics," Chris Chase/Yahoo Sports, last modified May 22, 2012. ca.sports.yahoo.com/blogs/olympics-fourth-place-medal/lolo-jones-says-remaining-virgin-harder-training-olympics – 171926254.html

Lie #4: Sex Is Okay as Long as It's Safe

a. US Department of Health and Human Services: Center for Disease Control and Prevention. "Sexually Transmitted Diseases (STDs) Prevention" homepage. Last modified November 15, 2011. www.cdc.gov/std/prevention/default.htm

b. US Department of Health and Human Services: Office of Adolescent Health. "Contraceptive and Condom Use," last modified January 16, 2013. www.hhs.gov/ash/oah/adolescent-health-topics/reproductive-health/contraceptive-use.html

Lie #8: I Need a Guy to Help Me Feel Complete

a. "Alleged 'Fix-a-Flat' fake surgeon Oneal Ron Morris arrested again after more victims come forward." Crimesider Staff, *CBS News*, March 14, 2012. www.cbsnews.com/8301 – 504083_162 – 57397200 – 504083/alleged-fix-a-flat-fake-surgeon-oneal-ron-morris-arrested-again-after-more-victims-come-forward/

Lie #9: Drawing Lines Doesn't Help Me Wait

a. US Department of Health and Human Services: Centers for Disease Control and Prevention. 2010. "Marriage and Cohabitation in the United States: A Statistical Portrait Based on Cycle 6 (2002) of the National Survey of Family Growth." *Vital and Health Statistics* 23 (28). www.cdc.gov/nchs/data/series/sr_23/sr23_028.pdf.

b. "With This Ring: A National Survey on Marriage in America." Norval D. Glenn, *National Fatherhood Initiative*, 2005. www.smartmarriages.com/nms.pdf.

c. John Regier. *Preparing for Marriage* (Caring for the Heart Ministries, 2010), page 112. Used with permission.

Lie #10: I Don't Have to Decide Now

a. "Reborn a Virgin: Adolescents' Retracting of Virginity Pledges and Sexual Histories," *American Journal of Public Health*, May 2, 2006, page 30.

MEET THE SPOTLIGHTS & THE QUOTABLES

Alex Schnee has always wanted to be a writer. She loves the smell of a bookstore, because nothing in the world smells exactly like it. She will never, ever like math and will always love dancing in the Montana rain. She is currently attending Sarah Lawrence College near New York City. Reach her at *alexinksit.com*.

Allison is a recent college grad who, like a few of the girls in this book, has asked to keep her identity anonymous. If you'd like to have mail forwarded to Allison, you can do so by sending it to Bekah at writebrained@gmail.com.

Annie Downs is an author/speaker who loves living in Nashville, Tennessee. Flawed but funny, she uses her writing to highlight the everyday goodness of a real and present God. Her first book, *Perfectly Unique* (Zondervan), uses real-life examples and faith-based instruction to equip Christian girls with the confidence, faith, and moxie they'll need to face their teen and college years. Find out more at *annieblogs.com*.

Betsy St. Amant is one good girl who enjoys writing about bad boys in her young adult novels. She lives in Louisiana with her fireman hubby and an adorable toddler who is already smarter than her author mom. Betsy is often found consuming massive amounts of chocolate and is an avid reader who is constantly wondering where Mr. Darcy went. A freelance journalist and fiction author, Betsy has a BA in Christian communications and is multipublished through Steeple Hill romances. Her first young adult novel, *Addison Blakely, Confessions of a PK* (Barbour), was released in 2012. Visit her at *betsystamant.com*.

Camy Tang grew up in Hawaii and now lives in Northern California with her engineer husband and rambunctious dog. She graduated from Stanford University and was a biologist researcher, but now she writes full-time. She is a staff worker for her church youth group and leads one of the Sunday worship teams. Visit her website at *camytang.com* to read free short stories and subscribe to her quarterly newsletter.

Denise Hildreth Jones's novels have moved her readers to tears and laughter as they stay up all night to finish the last page. "I'm just a southern girl from South Carolina who knows crazy people, the South, and rigged beauty pageants. So I thought I'd write a book about them. I didn't even know I could write fiction. Come to find out, people have fallen in love with that crazy *Savannah from Savannah* (Thomas Nelson), and I've fallen in love with telling stories." Learn more at *denisehildrethjones.com*.

Erynn Mangum is the author of more than ten books, including her most recent young adult novel, *Sketchy Behavior* (Zondervan). Learn more at *erynnmangum.com*.

Holley Gerth is the bestselling author of *You're Already Amazing* (Revell). She loves sharing her heart with women, drinking coffee, being with her husband, Mark, and living for Jesus (just not in that order). You're invited to hang out at her little place online, *holleygerth.com*.

Jan Kern lives in Northern California, serving alongside her husband at a residential ministry for at-risk youth. She is the author of *Scars That Wound, Scars That Heal — A Journey Out of Self-Injury* (Standard), an ECPA Gold Medallion finalist. As an author, speaker, and credentialed life coach, she encourages giving space for discovery and creativity, and for deeper conversation and connection —

with God and with others. Connect with Jan through her website, *jankern.com*.

Jenness Walker is an author and a book freak. Her first novel, *Double Take* (Steeple Hill), was released in 2009. *Bliss* (Written World Communications), coauthored with Tracy Bowen, followed in 2010. You can learn more about Jenness at *jennesswalker.com*.

Jessica is a writer and counselor who would prefer to keep her identity anonymous. If you'd like to have mail forwarded to Jess, you can contact her through Bekah at writebrained@gmail.com.

Kristin Billerbeck graduated from San Jose State University with a degree in journalism and mass communications, gave her life to Jesus during college, and found her true love in a Christian singles group, which she skewers in her book *What a Girl Wants* (Thomas Nelson). Together Kristin and her husband have four children. You can learn more about Kristin at *kristinbillerbeck.com*.

Lynn Martin Cowell is a Proverbs 31 Ministries speaker and the author of *His Revolutionary Love* (Standard), a book that helps girls develop higher self-esteem by discovering Christ's life-altering love. Learn more at *lynncowell.com*.

Madison has asked to keep her identity anonymous, but if you'd like to have mail forwarded to her, you can contact Bekah at writebrained@gmail.com.

Mary DeMuth is the author of more than a dozen books, including *Everything: What You Gain and What You Give to Become Like Jesus* (Thomas Nelson). She has spoken around the world, helping people live uncaged lives. Mary lives in Texas with her husband and three teens. Find out more at *MaryDeMuth.com*.

Melissa Nesdahl is the coauthor of *Nobody Told Me* (with Pam Stenzel, Regal) and *Who's in Your Social Network?* (with Pam Stenzel, Regal). She and her husband make their home in South Dakota, where she loves being Mama to three beautiful girls by day and writer by night. Find out more at *melissanesdahl.blogspot.com*.

Pam Stenzel is the founder of Enlighten Communications, an organization that empowers parents, youth leaders, and educators to lead informed discussions on sexual abstinence and its benefits. She speaks to over 500,000 teens a year and has coauthored *Nobody Told Me* and *Who's In Your Social Network?* with Melissa Nesdahl (Regal). Find more at *pamstenzel.com*.

Sarah Siebert Markley is a mother of two daughters (ages ten and sixteen) and has been married to her husband, Chad, for sixteen years. Sarah and her husband have been living a second-chance life of recovery, healing, and ministry after she confessed to an extramarital affair. Sarah is a monthly columnist for both *(in)courage. me* and *deeperstory.com* and writes regularly on her own blog at *sarahmarkley.com*. She's a speaker and a writer who believes that life is best lived with intention, grace, and the knowledge that every moment is precious.

Shannon Primicerio's books and conferences provide strategies for battling peer pressure in dating, purity, and friendship; insight on how to see yourself as a beautiful treasure; and direction on finding your purpose and living for the glory of God. You can learn more about Shannon at *beingagirlbooks.com*.

Stephanie Dixon's name was changed to protect her identity. If you'd like to have mail forwarded to Stephanie, you can contact her through Bekah at writebrained@gmail.com.

Stephanie Morrill is a twentysomething living in Overland Park, Kansas, with her husband and two kids. Stephanie is the author of The Reinvention of Skylar Hoyt series (Revell) and is currently working on other young adult projects. She enjoys encouraging and teaching teen writers on her blog, *GoTeenWriters.com*. To connect with Stephanie and read samples of her books, check out *StephanieMorrillBooks.com*.

Susie Shellenberger is an author and the editor of *Sisterhood Magazine*. You can learn more at *susiemagazine.com*.

Tabetha Brown grew up in Virginia and now lives in North Carolina with her husband, David, and son, Noah. She is a graphic designer and avid photographer. She has a heart for youth and loves to encourage people not to get caught up in the world but to live their lives devoted to Christ. She can be contacted at *www.facebook.com/tabetha.t.brown*.

Tracy Bowen is a transplanted southern gal who started writing women's fiction to counterbalance all the testosterone that surrounds her in the form of a husband and four sons. You can learn more about Tracy at *www.tandjbooks.blogspot.com*.

Tricia Goyer is the author of thirty-four books, including *Beside Still Waters* (B&H Books), *The Swiss Courier* (co-authored with Mike Yorkey, Revell), and the mommy memoir, *Blue Like Play Dough* (Multnomah). Tricia's book *Life Interrupted* (Zondervan) was a finalist for the Gold Medallion Award in 2005. In addition to her novels, Tricia writes nonfiction books and magazine articles for publications like *MomSense* and *Thriving Family*. She and her family make their home in Little Rock, Arkansas, where they are part of the ministry of FamilyLife. Visit *www.triciagoyer.com* for more about Tricia and her books.

T. Suzanne Eller is a Proverbs 31 Ministries speaker and author who lives in beautiful Oklahoma. She's a cancer survivor who loves life, God, and family, as well as hiking, rafting, and coming alongside women as they live free and full. Find out more at *www.tsuzanneeller.com.*

Sketchy Behavior

Erynn Mangum

Drawing Conclusions
or Drafting Disaster?

Other than harboring a somewhat obsessive fondness for
Crispix and completely swear-
ing-off boys after a bad date
(don't ask), sixteen-year-old
Kate Carter is about as ordinary as they come, except for her
two notable talents: art and sarcasm. After an introduction to
forensic sketching in her elective art class, Kate discovers a
third and most unexpected gift: criminal profiling. Her photo-
quality sketch helps the police catch a wanted murderer and
earns her celebrity status in South Woodhaven Falls. But when
that murderer appears to be using his friends to exact revenge,
Kate goes from local hero to possible target. Will she manage
to survive? Will life ever be normal again? And will local news
anchor Ted Deffle ever stop sending her flowers?

Available in stores and online!

Perfectly Unique

Praising God from Head to Foot

Annie F. Downs

Your body is an instrument. No, it's not a flute, or a guitar (I hope). It is a sacred and original design by a master craftsman with a specific plan and purpose. That's a pretty big deal.

From head to foot, the way you view your body is directly connected to how you serve God. Seriously. From the thoughts you think to the steps you take, every part of you is linked to the divine.

Perhaps you are struggling with your body image or are trying to make sense of why God made you as you are. Maybe you are looking for new ways to understand Scripture or to love God more fully. Either way, this book will take you on a thoughtful, funny, and spirit-filled exploration of the way you were designed and will help you better honor the Creator by learning to value his perfectly unique creation (yourself!).

Talk It Up!

Want free books?
First looks at the best new fiction?
Awesome exclusive merchandise?

We want to hear from you!

Give us your opinions on titles, covers, and stories.
Join the Z Street Team.

Visit zstreetteam.zondervan.com/joinnow
to sign up today!

Also—Friend us on Facebook!

www.facebook.com/goodteenreads

- Video Trailers
- Connect with your favorite authors
- Sneak peeks at new releases
- Giveaways
- Fun discussions
- And much more!